AF897186

SUPREME® BAR REVIEW

Real Property

Bar Exam Review

Supreme Bar Review
30539 Pinetree Road, Suite 224
Cleveland, Ohio 44124

(866) BAR-PREP (toll-free)

SupremeBarReview.com

Printed in the United States of America.

ISBN-13: 978-1-936450-06-0

For information address:

Supreme Bar Review
30539 Pinetree Road, Suite 224
Cleveland, Ohio 44124

SupremeBarReview.com

TABLE OF CONTENTS

I. THE FREEHOLD ESTATES IN LAND

We continue to categorize interests in land as lawyers did at common law. Interests are classified according to their potential duration.

Watch Out!

There is a lot of potentially confusing terminology in the area of real property. If you do not know the difference between a "remainder" and "reversion" make a vocabulary list or flash cards and quiz yourself over and over until you know the key terminology.

Once you have mastered the language of real property, you will find it easier to eliminate wrong answer choices on the MBE, which will improve your chances of picking the right answer.

A. FEE SIMPLE ABSOLUTE

The estate with the longest potential duration and hence the greatest estate known to our law is the fee simple absolute. A fee simple absolute can last forever. It will end, generally, only if the holder of the estate dies without heirs and without making a testamentary disposition of his or her property. In such a case, the property held in fee simple will *escheat* to the state.

1. **Creation** - Conveyancers at common law used specific language to create a fee simple absolute that made clear the estate could be inherited by the holder's heirs. We continue to use that language today. A conveyance to "A and her heirs" gives A a fee simple absolute.

   Note: A's heirs receive nothing from the quoted grant. The phrase "and her heirs" connotes A is receiving a fee simple absolute. The phrase consists of *words of limitation* that describe the estate A receives. They are not *words of purchase* used to state who receives the property.

   Example: O conveys Blackacre to "A and her heirs." At the time of the conveyance, A has a daughter, B. A's creditors attach Blackacre and shortly thereafter A dies intestate. A's creditors will be able to sell Blackacre in satisfaction of their debts. The conveyance gave A a fee simple absolute that could be reached by his creditors. B did not receive any interest in Blackacre under the terms of O's grant. At the time she would have been entitled to inherit the estate it was already encumbered by the creditor's attachment.

   Modern Trend: Today, the law generally presumes a person conveys a fee simple absolute unless they clearly express a contrary intention. Thus, a conveyance of Blackacre "to A" without any words of limitation will be presumed to be a grant of a fee simple absolute to A.

2. **Attributes** - In addition to being *inheritable*, a fee simple absolute is *devisable* (i.e., it can be given to another through the terms of a will), and *alienable* (i.e., it can be sold, leased, given away or attached by one's creditors).

B. FEE TAIL

A fee tail was created at common law when an estate was made to last for as long as the grantee had lineal descendants. Remember that the term "heirs at law" includes anyone who will inherit the property of a decedent who dies intestate. The term can include uncle, aunts, nieces, nephews and quite distant cousins. A fee tail could not pass along any of these collateral lines, but could descend only in the grantee's direct line, i.e., children, grandchildren, great-grandchildren and so on.

1. **Creation** - The words of limitation used to create a fee tail were to "heirs of the grantee's body" or "to the grantee's issue." Thus, a grant "to A and the heirs of his body" would create a fee tail in A at common law.

2. **Future Interest** - Unlike a fee simple absolute, the grantor of a fee tail retains a future interest. If the grantee's line failed, that is, the grantee or one of his or her descendants died without issue, the property would revert back to the grantor. This future interest retained by the grantor following a fee tail was called a *reversion*.

3. **Attributes** - At common law, a fee tail could not pass out of the grantee's line. A person holding an entailed estate could only alienate their present possessory interest. The estate was not devisable nor inheritable to anyone other than the grantee's lineal descendants.

4. **Present Day Form** - Nearly every American jurisdiction has abolished the fee tail. In most states, if a grantor uses words that would have created an entailed estate at common law, the courts will construe the language to vest a fee simple in the donee.

C. THE LIFE ESTATE

When the duration of an estate is measured by a person's life, it is called a life estate.

1. **Creation** - Words of limitation that limit the duration of an estate to a lifetime create a life estate. Look for words like, "for life," or "for long as he shall live," etc.

2. **Future Interest**- The grantor of a life estate retains a reversion if the grantor does not give the future interest following the estate to a third party. If the future interest following a life estate is given to a person other that the grantor, it is called a *remainder*.

3. **Attributes** - The life tenant of a life estate can sell, lease or otherwise alienate their present possessory interest. The life tenant cannot alienate or otherwise dispose of the future interest following the estate. Thus, a life estate is not inheritable or devisable. A life estate can be measured by a life other than the life of the life tenant. In such a case, the estate is called a life estate *pur autre vie* or a life estate measured by the life of another.

Example: O grants Blackacre to A for life. A later sells all her right title and interest in Blackacre to B. At that time, B holds a life estate *pur autre vie*, which will last as long as A lives. O has a reversion.

D. FEE SIMPLE DETERMINABLE

Any present possessory estate can be made determinable if it ends automatically upon the happening of a stated event with title to revert back to the grantor. While we will focus on determinable fees, remember life estates can be made determinable as well.

1. **Creation** - A fee simple determinable can be created with words of limitation that indicate the estate ends automatically upon the happening of a stated condition with title to immediately revert to the grantor.

   Example: Thus, a grant "to A for so long as the property is used as a school" creates a fee simple determinable in A. Similar words, i.e., "until," "during," "only while," may also indicate the grantor intends the estate to end automatically upon the happening of a stated event and therefore will also create a fee simple determinable.

   The grantor who wishes to create a fee simple determinable must use clear language of condition. Words that only indicate the grantor's motive or purpose in making the grant will not suffice to create the estate. Thus, a grant "to A for use as a school" would be construed by many courts as a grant of a fee simple absolute to A with the grantor only indicating his motive in making the grant.

2. **Future Interest -** The future interest retained by the grantor of a determinable fee is called a *possibility of reverter.*

3. **Attributes -** A determinable fee is *inheritable*, *devisable*, and freely *alienable*. Anyone succeeding to a fee simple determinable, of course, takes the estate subject to a possibility of defeaseance if the operative event occurs. In the above example, if A sells his interest in the property to B, and B ceases to use the property as a school, title will revert back to A's original grantor.

E. FEE SIMPLE ON A CONDITION SUBSEQUENT

An estate on a condition subsequent arises when the grantor of a defeasible estate retains a right to reenter and take possession of the property from the grantee if a stated condition occurs. The estate differs from a determinable estate in that the present possessory interest does not end automatically. The grantor must exercise a retained power to terminate the grantee's estate.

1. **Creation** - A fee simple on a condition subsequent is created when words of limitation are used that indicate the grantor has retained the right to reenter or terminate the grantee's estate if a stated condition occurs.

Example: O would create a fee simple on a condition subsequent if he grants property "to A for use as a school but if A should ever cease to use the property for school purposes then O shall have the right to reenter." Courts will generally construe language of condition as a grant of a fee simple on a condition subsequent. Look for words like "on condition that," "provided that," and "but if ...then."

2. **Future Interest** - The future interest retained by the grantor following a fee simple on a condition subsequent is called a *right of entry* or *power of termination.*

3. **Attributes** - Like the fee simple determinable, a fee simple on a condition subsequent is *alienable, devisable* and *inheritable.*

F. FEE SIMPLE SUBJECT TO EXECUTORY LIMITATION

An estate can be made defeasible and have the future interest following the estate pass to a third person other than the grantor. In such a case we say the estate is subject to an executory limitation.

1. **Creation -** A fee simple subject to an executory limitation is created by any language that states the fee will end upon the happening of a stated event followed by a future interest in a third person. It does not matter whether the divesting condition is phrased in determinable or conditional form. In either case, the present possessory fee is called a fee simple subject to an executory limitation. The key feature is the future interest in a third person.

   Example: O conveys Blackacre "to A and her heirs but if B should become a member of the state bar then to B and his heirs." A has a fee simple subject to an executory limitation. B has an *executory interest.*

2. **Future Interest -** The future interest in a third person that follows a fee simple on an executory limitation is an *executory interest.*

3. **Attributes -** Like the other defeasible fees, a fee simple subject to an executory limitation is *alienable, devisable* and *inheritable.*

II. FUTURE INTERESTS

Those interests in property that are not presently possessory are called future interests. They fall into two broad categories, future interests retained by the grantor of a present possessory estate and future interests given to third parties.

A. FUTURE INTERESTS IN THE GRANTOR

A grantor can retain three future interests:

1. **Possibility of Reverter -** If the grantor has conveyed a determinable estate such as a fee simple determinable, the grantor retains a possibility of reverter. Remember a possibility of reverter only follows a determinable estate. Do not confuse the term with a reversion. Possibilities of reverter are alienable, inheritable and devisable.

2. **Right of Entry or Power of Termination** - The future interest retained by a grantor who has conveyed a present possessory interest on a condition subsequent is called either a right of entry or a power of termination.

   Common Law: At common law, some courts treated rights of entry like choses in action. They therefore would not permit a holder of a right of entry to sell or otherwise transfer them *inter vivos.*

   Modern Trend: Today, those restrictions on alienability have largely been abolished and rights of entry are fully alienable, inheritable and devisable.

3. **Reversion** - Any other future interest retained by the grantor is called a reversion. The grantor retains a reversion anytime the grantor has conveyed away less than a vested remainder in fee simple absolute. Reversions can be sold, given away or otherwise alienated, devised and inherited.

B. FUTURE INTEREST IN THIRD PARTIES

There are two general categories of future interests in third parties – remainders and executory interests:

1. **Remainders** - Remainders are future interests in third parties that become possessory upon the natural termination of the preceding estate. They do not divest or otherwise cut the preceding estate short. They also must become possessory immediately upon the termination of the preceding estate.

2. **Executory Interests** - If a future interest in a third party divests a preceding interest or fails to become possessory immediately upon its termination, it is an executory interest, not a remainder.

   Example: A grant "to A for life and then to B" creates a life estate in A and a remainder in B.

   Example: A grant "to A for life and one year later to B" creates a life estate in A, a reversion in the grantor, and an executory interest in B.

   Example: A grant "to A for life and then to B and his heirs, but if C passes the bar exam after A's death, to C and her heirs" gives A a life estate, B a remainder and C an executory interest.

C. VESTED AND CONTINGENT REMAINDERS

A remainder is *contingent* if it is either given to an unascertained person or it is subject to a condition precedent. Conversely, a remainder is *vested* if it is given to an ascertained person and is otherwise not subject to any such condition.

Example: O grants Blackacre "to A for life, remainder to A's children." If A has no children, the remainder to them would be contingent. They are unascertained.

Example: A grant to A for life and then to B and her heirs if B passes the bar examination is contingent. B's remainder is subject to the condition precedent that she passes the exam.

Example: A grant to A for life, then to B for life, then to C for life creates a life estate in A, a vested remainder in a life estate in B and a vested remainder in a life estate in C. B and C both have vested remainders because their interests will become possessory upon the termination of the preceding estate and are not subject to any other condition. In this example, the grantor retains a reversion. Why? The grantor has not conveyed a vested remainder in fee simple absolute.

D. SHIFTING AND SPRINGING EXECUTORY INTERESTS

Remember executory interests differ from remainders in that they divest a prior transferee. If an executory interest divests the grantor, we call it a *springing executory interest.* If it divests another grantee, we call it a *shifting executory interest.*

Example: In the example given above of a grant "to A for life and then to B and his heirs, but if C passes the bar examination after A's death, to C and her heirs," C has a shifting executory interest. It is shifting because it divests a prior transferee, B.

Example: A grant "to A for life, and one year after A's death, to B and his heirs" gives B a *springing executory interest.* He will divest the reversion in the grantor that follows the termination of A's life estate.

E. REMAINDERS SUBJECT TO PARTIAL OR COMPLETE DIVESTMENT

As some of the earlier examples illustrate, a remainder can be cut short by an executory interest. We say such a remainder is *subject to divestment* or *defeasance.* In some cases, a remainder is subject to only partial divestment. The typical case involves a remainder given to a class of persons. The remainder may be vested as to some members of the class but others may yet enter the class and share in the remainder. We call such a remainder *subject to open* or *subject to partial divestment.*

Example: O devises Blackacre "to A for life, remainder to A's children." At O's death A has two children B and C. The children, B and C, have vested remainders. They are both ascertained persons and the devise imposes no conditions precedent on their taking their remainder. Because A is still alive, however, A may have additional children. Those children will enter the class of persons devised the remainder. Therefore, B and C have vested remainders subject to open or subject to partial divestment.

Example: In the example we have seen before of a grant "to A for life and then to B and his heirs, but if C passes the bar examination after A's death, to C and her heirs," B's remainder is subject to complete divestment or defeasance. When C passes the bar, her executory interest will become possessory as a fee simple to the complete exclusion of B.

Example: A grant to A for life and then to B and his heirs creates a vested remainder in B or, if we wished to underscore that no executory interest will divest it, we could say B's remainder was *indefeasably vested.*

F. ATTRIBUTES

Remainders and executory interests are generally fully alienable, devisable and inheritable. These interests are subject to a number of rules, however, including the rule against perpetuities, that have the effect of clearing titles of future interests that impair the marketability of land.

III. THE NON-FREEHOLD ESTATES AND THE LAW OF LANDLORD AND TENANT

The non-freehold estates are leaseholds. In a leasehold estate, the tenant enjoys all rights attendant with possession for the term of the lease. At common law, a lease was very much considered a conveyance of real property. While that is still true today, the law of landlord and tenant has borrowed heavily in recent decades from the law of contracts. Both courts and legislatures have recently reformed many aspects of the common law of landlord and tenant This outline uses the terms *landlord* and *tenant.* Legal synonyms for these terms are *lessor* and *lessee* respectively.

A. THE NON-FREEHOLD ESTATES

There are four types of non-freehold estates:

1. **The Estate for Years -** An estate or tenancy for years is created when the leasehold lasts for a fixed term. The term of the lease, in other words, has a definite starting date and ending date. The estate is badly named because a tenancy for any fixed duration is still called an estate for years. An estate for years, for example, can be for a week, two weeks, six months, twenty years or any other fixed period of time.

   Common Law: The English Statute of Frauds (1677) required leases for three years or longer to be in writing.

   Modern Trend: Most contemporary statutes require a signed writing for leases longer than a year. The statute of frauds and its exceptions are discussed in more detail, *infra.*

   An estate for years ends when the defined term expires. Neither the landlord nor the tenant is required to give the other notice of termination.

2. **The Periodic Tenancy** - A periodic tenancy is a leasehold of no fixed duration. It arises when term of the lease is defined by a period that repeats itself, as for example, a tenancy from month to month or year to year. Absent notice of termination, a periodic tenancy may last indefinitely.

   At common law, a party desiring to terminate a periodic tenancy had to give the other party notice of termination equal to the period but not exceeding six months. Thus, a landlord or a tenant could terminate a tenancy from month to month on one month's notice. A party was required to give six months notice to terminate a year to year lease. The common law required notice of termination on the last day of the period or the notice was ineffective. Thus, notice to terminate a month to month lease that began on the first of the month, had to be given on the last day of the month.

   Example: A leased Blackacre to B on a month to month lease beginning January 1st. On July 5th, B gave A notice of termination. Most courts would hold the notice was ineffective to terminate the lease before August 31st.

   Courts will often infer the intent of the parties, to create a periodic tenancy from the rental term.

   Example: Consider a lease agreement that establishes no fixed term but provides that rent is payable on the first of each month. A court would likely view the tenancy as a periodic tenancy from month to month.

3. **The Tenancy At Will -** A tenancy at will has no fixed term and is terminable by either party at anytime. The parties must expressly agree to a tenancy at will. The courts will rarely find a tenancy at will absent very clear language in the lease agreement because the tenancy is so precarious for both parties.

   Common Law: At common law, no advance notice was required to terminate a tenancy at will.

   Modern Trend: By statute or judicial decision, states have established a requirement of reasonable notice. A tenancy at will ended with the death of the landlord or tenant converting the tenancy into a tenancy at sufferance.

4. **The Tenancy At Sufferance or Holdover Tenant -** A tenancy at sufferance exists when the tenant is in possession of the leasehold without the landlord's agreement or acquiescence. It usually arises when a tenant "holds over" after the termination of earlier lease.

   A landlord faced with a holdover tenant could elect to treat the holdover tenant as if the tenant had agreed to a new tenancy equal in duration to that of the original lease. Alternatively, the landlord may evict the holdover tenant and recover damages for trespass.

Generally, a constructive eviction cannot arise from the acts of third parties. However, if the landlord has some control over the acts giving rise to a claim of constructive eviction liability may result.

Example: A leased an apartment to B under the terms of a standard form lease that prohibited the tenant from playing loud music or otherwise disturbing the quiet of the house between 10:00 p.m. and 10:00 a.m. A neighbor of B's, C, constantly played her stereo at all hours. After several ineffectual complaints, B vacates. A constructive eviction may be attributed to A for failure to enforce the terms of C's lease requiring quiet hours.

Both residential and commercial tenants may raise a claim of constructive eviction.

c. **Partial Eviction -** An eviction can be *partial* where the tenant has been deprived of the use and enjoyment of only a portion of the leased premises. In a partial actual eviction by the landlord or his agents, the courts generally excuse the tenant from paying any rent, even for the portion of the premises the tenant occupies. The courts reason that the landlord should not be able to apportion a wrong.

Example: A leases a commercial warehouse from B. When he takes possession, he notices that B is using a quarter of the space to store B's equipment. B does not remove his equipment. A has been partially evicted and B has materially breached the lease.

There is yet little authority for a finding a partial constructive eviction but there have been recent cases which have allowed a tenant to pay a reduced rent when the tenant has been constructively evicted from a portion of the leasehold.

3. **Abandonment of Possession** - A tenant *abandons* a leasehold if the tenant fails to pay rent and vacates the premises without justification and without the intention to return. An abandonment is a material breach of lease by the tenant.

4. **Duty to Mitigate** - At common law, a landlord was under no duty to re-let the premises if a tenant had abandoned a leasehold. The tenant remained liable for rent throughout the term of the lease. In recent years, many courts have required a landlord to mitigate damages caused by a tenant's abandonment. These courts have generally required a landlord to treat an abandoned unit as the landlord would any other vacate unit, i.e, advertise the unit for rent and show it to prospective tenants. If the landlord re-lets the premises, the tenant is liable for any difference in rent received by the landlord as well as the landlord's incidental expenses incurred in re-letting the premises. If a landlord has failed to make reasonable efforts to mitigate, the defaulting tenant's damages may be reduced by the amount of rent the landlord could have obtained by re-letting the premises for the remainder of the term.

Courts have excused tenants who have held over due to extenuating cir as the tenant's serious illness. Courts also have found that landlords ha tenant's holding over, as for example, by accepting rent. Either by stat a lease, a tenant may be liable for double rent or other charges for holdi courts rule that such statutes or express lease provisions govern a dispu holding over rather than the common law remedies.

B. POSSESSION

A lease was largely understood at common law as a conveyance of the use real property, in other words, the right to possession. The landlord's duty t uninterrupted possession to the tenant remains the landlord's primary oblig lease.

1. **Delivery of Possession** - At one time, many American jurisdictions hel had only a duty to deliver to a tenant the legal right to possession at the of the lease term. Under this older view, the landlord did not have to del possession to the tenant. Modern decisions have made this a minority v jurisdictions now hold the landlord must deliver actual possession to the

   Example: A leases Blackacre to B. At the commencement of the term, hold over tenant, C, is still in possession. At common law, under the so- rule, there would be no breach of lease on A's part. A had conveyed to possession superior to C's right. Under the modern view, however, A h obligation, implied in the lease, to deliver actual possession to B.

2. **Interference with the Right of Possession** - A covenant of *quiet enjoym* every lease agreement. The covenant is breached if the tenant's possessi by the landlord, anyone claiming through the landlord, or anyone with a the premises. If the tenant is evicted as a result, the tenant's obligations including the obligation to pay rent, comes to an end. Moreover, the lan liable to the tenant for damages. An eviction can be actual, constructive

   a. **Actual Eviction** - An actual eviction occurs when the landlord, the la or someone with a superior title ousts the tenant.

   b. **Constructive Eviction** - A constructive eviction occurs when the ten enjoyment of the leasehold has been substantially interfered with by t the landlord's agents. The deprivation must be serious enough to cau vacate the premises reasonably promptly. A constructive eviction exc obligation to pay rent.

      Example: In September, A leases an apartment to B for a year. In ea the blower in the central furnace breaks down. As a result, B's apartn inadequate heat. B notifies A, but A does not fix the blower. B vacat December. B is excused from the obligation to pay rent.

Courts have excused tenants who have held over due to extenuating circumstances such as the tenant's serious illness. Courts also have found that landlords have consented to a tenant's holding over, as for example, by accepting rent. Either by statute or by terms of a lease, a tenant may be liable for double rent or other charges for holding over. Usually courts rule that such statutes or express lease provisions govern a dispute over a tenant holding over rather than the common law remedies.

B. POSSESSION

A lease was largely understood at common law as a conveyance of the use and enjoyment of real property, in other words, the right to possession. The landlord's duty to deliver uninterrupted possession to the tenant remains the landlord's primary obligation under a lease.

1. **Delivery of Possession** - At one time, many American jurisdictions held that a landlord had only a duty to deliver to a tenant the legal right to possession at the commencement of the lease term. Under this older view, the landlord did not have to deliver actual possession to the tenant. Modern decisions have made this a minority view. Most jurisdictions now hold the landlord must deliver actual possession to the tenant.

   Example: A leases Blackacre to B. At the commencement of the term, B discovers a hold over tenant, C, is still in possession. At common law, under the so-called American rule, there would be no breach of lease on A's part. A had conveyed to B a right to possession superior to C's right. Under the modern view, however, A has breached the obligation, implied in the lease, to deliver actual possession to B.

2. **Interference with the Right of Possession** - A covenant of *quiet enjoyment* is implied in every lease agreement. The covenant is breached if the tenant's possession is disturbed by the landlord, anyone claiming through the landlord, or anyone with a superior claim to the premises. If the tenant is evicted as a result, the tenant's obligations under the lease, including the obligation to pay rent, comes to an end. Moreover, the landlord may be liable to the tenant for damages. An eviction can be actual, constructive or partial:

   a. Actual Eviction - An actual eviction occurs when the landlord, the landlord's agent or someone with a superior title ousts the tenant.

   b. Constructive Eviction - A constructive eviction occurs when the tenant's use and enjoyment of the leasehold has been substantially interfered with by the landlord or the landlord's agents. The deprivation must be serious enough to cause the tenant to vacate the premises reasonably promptly. A constructive eviction excuses the obligation to pay rent.

   Example: In September, A leases an apartment to B for a year. In early November, the blower in the central furnace breaks down. As a result, B's apartment receives inadequate heat. B notifies A, but A does not fix the blower. B vacates in mid-December. B is excused from the obligation to pay rent.

Generally, a constructive eviction cannot arise from the acts of third parties. However, if the landlord has some control over the acts giving rise to a claim of constructive eviction liability may result.

Example: A leased an apartment to B under the terms of a standard form lease that prohibited the tenant from playing loud music or otherwise disturbing the quiet of the house between 10:00 p.m. and 10:00 a.m. A neighbor of B's, C, constantly played her stereo at all hours. After several ineffectual complaints, B vacates. A constructive eviction may be attributed to A for failure to enforce the terms of C's lease requiring quiet hours.

Both residential and commercial tenants may raise a claim of constructive eviction.

c. **Partial Eviction -** An eviction can be *partial* where the tenant has been deprived of the use and enjoyment of only a portion of the leased premises. In a partial actual eviction by the landlord or his agents, the courts generally excuse the tenant from paying any rent, even for the portion of the premises the tenant occupies. The courts reason that the landlord should not be able to apportion a wrong.

Example: A leases a commercial warehouse from B. When he takes possession, he notices that B is using a quarter of the space to store B's equipment. B does not remove his equipment. A has been partially evicted and B has materially breached the lease.

There is yet little authority for a finding a partial constructive eviction but there have been recent cases which have allowed a tenant to pay a reduced rent when the tenant has been constructively evicted from a portion of the leasehold.

3. **Abandonment of Possession** - A tenant *abandons* a leasehold if the tenant fails to pay rent and vacates the premises without justification and without the intention to return. An abandonment is a material breach of lease by the tenant.

4. **Duty to Mitigate** - At common law, a landlord was under no duty to re-let the premises if a tenant had abandoned a leasehold. The tenant remained liable for rent throughout the term of the lease. In recent years, many courts have required a landlord to mitigate damages caused by a tenant's abandonment. These courts have generally required a landlord to treat an abandoned unit as the landlord would any other vacate unit, i.e, advertise the unit for rent and show it to prospective tenants. If the landlord re-lets the premises, the tenant is liable for any difference in rent received by the landlord as well as the landlord's incidental expenses incurred in re-letting the premises. If a landlord has failed to make reasonable efforts to mitigate, the defaulting tenant's damages may be reduced by the amount of rent the landlord could have obtained by re-letting the premises for the remainder of the term.

5. **Surrender of Possession** - A *surrender* is the landlord's acceptance of a tenant's relinquishment of possession before the end of the lease term. If the landlord accepts a surrender, the lease comes to an end and the tenant is not liable for rent for the remainder of the lease term. The landlord's intent is a critical issue in surrender cases. Remember the landlord may and, today, frequently must, attempt to re-let an abandoned leasehold. The landlord should make his or her intention clear that any efforts undertaken to re-let the premises are made to reduce the tenant's damages and do not constitute acceptance of a surrender.

6. **Recovery of Possession** - At common law, a landlord could use self-help to recover possession of a leasehold in the event of a breach by the tenant of the obligation to pay rent or any other material condition of the lease. In exercising the right of self-help, however, the landlord could not use force to enter the leasehold or bar the tenant from entry, a crime known as forcible entry and detainer. Today, most states have authorized summary eviction proceedings for a failure to pay rent and have prohibited self-help of any kind.

7. **Rent** - The tenant's primary obligation under a lease is the payment of rent. At common law, a tenant's obligation to pay rent was generally only excused by an eviction. Today, courts have increasingly treated a lease as a contract and the tenant's obligation to pay rent may be excused in whole or in part under doctrines borrowed from the law of contracts.

    a. **Acceleration and Anticipatory Repudiation** - If the tenant fails to pay rent, the landlord is entitled to sue for any amounts past due. What has been more problematic are the rents to be paid under the lease that are not yet due. At common law, a landlord could not use the contract doctrine of anticipatory repudiation to recover rent not yet due. As a result the landlord could either: (i) evict the tenant; or (ii) allow the tenant to remain in possession and sue for each installment of the rent as it became due.

       Modern Trend: Today, most courts will allow a landlord to enforce a lease by suing for the unpaid rent and the present value of future rentals. The courts will also enforce an *acceleration* clause, that provides all rent due under a lease is payable upon default of any installment.

    b. **Destruction of the Leased Premises** - At common law, destruction of the leased premises by fire, war, earthquake or other catastrophic event, did not excuse a tenant from the obligation to pay rent. The courts at common law reasoned the right to possession of the land was paramount. Structures were not the heart of the bargain. An exception developed from this line of reasoning, however. If a tenant leased only a portion of a building, destruction of the building ended the obligation to pay rent. In such a case, the courts were willing to say that occupancy of the building was a central part of the tenant's bargain.

Modern Trend: Today, courts generally employ contract law doctrines like impossibility of performance or frustration of purpose to excuse the obligation to pay rent if the leased premises are destroyed.

c. **The Doctrine of Independent Covenants** - The doctrine of independent covenants was one of the central reasons the common law courts so seldom excused the obligation of a tenant to pay rent. Under the doctrine, the obligations of a landlord and a tenant were considered independent of one another so that the breach of one promise in a lease did not excuse the obligation to perform another promise set forth in the lease.

Modern Trend: Today, courts increasingly treat lease agreements as contracts in which the promises made by the parties are dependent. A material breach by one party to the lease will excuse the obligation of the other to perform. The issue frequently arises today in disputes over the condition of the leased premises.

8. **Condition of the Leased Premises** - At common law, the Latin phrase, *caveat lessee*, largely summed up the law regarding a landlord's duties with respect to the condition of the leasehold. Absent a contrary agreement in the lease, a landlord was generally not responsible for the condition of the leased premises. The landlord had no duty to repair or maintain the premises. By and large, this is no longer the law with regard to residential leases.

a. **Housing Codes** - In the nineteenth century, jurisdictions began to adopt housing codes in an effort to address the problem of slum housing. These Codes set forth minimum standards for the conditions of rental housing. The Codes are enforced administratively and are generally not understood to create a private right of action. A few jurisdictions have, however, allowed a tenant who was sued for rent to raise the contract defense of illegality by claiming the condition of the leased premises violated the Housing Code.

b. **Warranty of Habitability** - A more far-reaching reform of the common law took place when the courts and state legislatures began to recognize an implied warranty of habitability in every residential lease. Under the implied warranty a landlord has a continuing duty to provide and maintain premises fit for human habitation. At a minimum, the warranty requires landlords to comply with the material provisions of any applicable building, health or safety code.

1) Remedies for Breach - If a residential tenant notifies a landlord of a defect in the condition of the leased premises that amounts to a breach of the warranty of habitability and the landlord fails to repair the defect, the law today generally permits a tenant to: (1) refuse to pay rent or pay it into court until the defect is repaired; (2) terminate the lease; (3) raise the breach as a defense to an action for rent or summary eviction; or (4) repair the defect and deduct the costs of the repair against the rent.

A tenant is not required to vacate the leased premises in order to claim a breach of the warranty of habitability as the tenant is required to do in order to claim a constructive eviction.

2) **Disclaimers** - Most states refuse to enforce any disclaimer of the warranty of habitability in the lease or otherwise. The warranty of habitability cannot be waived.

3) **Leaseholds Covered by the Warranty** - The warranty of habitability generally extends only to residential tenancies, not commercial leases.

9. **Retaliatory Eviction** - A landlord may not retaliate against a tenant who complains about the condition of the leased premises either to the landlord or to housing authorities. At a minimum, this means the landlord may not raise the tenant's rent, threaten an eviction or deprive the tenant of services as a result of a complaint.

10. **Tort Liability** - At common law, the tenant was responsible for keeping the leasehold premises safe for others. At common law the tenant's duty of care varied depending upon whether the person on the premises was an invitee, licensee or trespasser. Today, the tenant is generally held to owe a duty of reasonable care under the circumstances to all persons on the premises.

While a landlord at common law had no duty to maintain a leasehold in a safe condition, the general rule was subject to a number of exceptions. These exceptions largely govern a landlord's liability today:

a. **Common Areas** - A landlord is generally held responsible for the condition of stairways, halls, entrances, parking garages and other common areas of a building.

b. **Latent Defects** - The landlord is generally held liable for injuries resulting from latent defects, i.e., those not obvious on visual inspection, *if the landlord knew or should have known of the defect.* A corollary rule is, a landlord is not responsible for obvious or patent defects.

c. **Responsibility Undertaken** - If a landlord agrees in a lease to maintain the premises, the landlord may be liable for failure to do so with due care. Similarly, if the landlord undertakes a repair, the landlord is liable if the repair is performed negligently.

d. **Public Use** - If the landlord is aware that all or part of the premises will be open to the public, the landlord must correct all conditions that pose a danger to the public if the landlord knows or should know of the condition, the condition exists at the beginning of the lease term, and the landlord has no reason to expect the tenant will repair it.

e. **Acts of Third Parties** - Generally, one is not responsible for the intentional torts of a third party. Some recent cases, however, have held a landlord liable for criminal assaults on leased premises, if the assaults were foreseeable and avoidable by some action taken by the landlord.

Example: A number of criminal assaults have occurred in the hallway of an apartment building owned by A. The hallway is easily accessible to the street and poorly lighted. B, a tenant of A, is assaulted in the hallway by C. A may be liable for B's resulting injuries even though their immediate cause was B's intentional tort.

11. **Provisions in the Lease** – Provisions in a lease may alter a party's responsibility for repairs and the condition of the premises. A lease agreement may also provide for a security deposit to protect the landlord if the tenant does not maintain the premises, pay rent or otherwise faithfully perform the terms and conditions of the lease.

a. **Exculpatory Clauses** – A landlord may seek to avoid liability in tort through an exculpatory clause in the lease. Such a clause obviously cannot be enforced against a third party who did not join in the lease. Courts are also increasingly unwilling to enforce the clause against an injured tenant. If a landlord has a duty to repair or maintain some condition of the premises under the rules outlined above, the courts will not enforce a clause designed to shield the landlord from liability for the landlord's own negligence in performing that duty.

b. **Repair Clause** – A lease agreement may, however, shift who has a duty of repair in some circumstances. The courts will enforce a clause in the lease that requires a tenant to make all repairs, if the clause does not have the effect of waiving the warranty of habitability. Such a clause usually does not, however, shift a risk of catastrophic loss to the tenant.

Example: A leased a farmhouse and the surrounding acreage to B for a term of five years. The lease required B to keep the premises in good repair. Two years into the term, a tornado destroyed the house. Absent more express language in the lease, the repair clause will not shift risk of the loss to the tenant.

c. **Security Deposits** – A lease may require the tenant to pay the landlord a deposit to assure the payment of rent, proper maintenance of the leasehold and any other obligation of the tenant under the lease. Generally, a landlord may not retain the full amount of a security deposit if the amount of any unpaid rent or damage to the premises is less than the amount of the deposit. In such a case, the landlord must return any excess to the tenant. *See, e.g.* ***Heyman v. Linwood Park, Inc.***, 41 N.J.Super. 437 (1956). If the lease characterizes the amount of a security deposit as liquidated damages, the standard rules of contract law apply. The liquidated damage provision is enforceable if the amount is a reasonable approximation of the actual damages the landlord would incur as a consequence of the breach. At common law, a landlord had no duty to pay interest on a security deposit. In most states, however, statutes regulate security deposits today. Typical statutes limit the amount of deposits and require the payment of interest, particularly if the deposit is held for a year or more. Statutes frequently require a landlord to describe in writing the reasons he or she has kept a deposit and to itemize the amounts retained.

12. **Transfer of Rights Under a Lease** - The law favors free alienability of property rights. Thus, both a tenant and a landlord are free to transfer their rights under a lease absent a contrary provision in the lease agreement.

   a. **Transfer of the Landlord's Interest** - A landlord may assign the landlord's interest under a lease. This typically occurs when the landlord sells the real property subject to the lease. The assignee in such a transaction acquires the rights and assumes the duties of the landlord under the lease.

      1) **Claims and Defenses** - As with the law of contracts generally, an assignee takes subject to all contract claims and defenses that were good against the assignor:

         Example: A sells his apartment building to B. A does not disclose to B the condition of the plumbing in an apartment leased to C. The plumbing is unhealthy and C has demanded that A repair it. When B seeks to collect rent from C, a defense of breach of the warranty of habitability may be raised by C. It does not matter that B did not know of the unhealthy condition or of C's complaint. B takes the lease subject to any defenses that would be good against A.

      2) **Attornment** - An assignee of a landlord may ask the existing tenants in a building to affirm the terms of their leases with a document known as an **attornment** certificate. A tenant who signs such a certificate may be barred from asserting a defense against the assignee which the tenant could have asserted against the original landlord.

         Example: A occupies an apartment in a building owned by B. A's written lease is year to year but B orally promised not to raise A's rent for a period of five years. B agrees to sell the building to C. C asks the tenants of the building to sign certificates affirming the terms of their leases. A signs such a certificate. When C renews A's lease the next year, C should be able to raise A's rent notwithstanding A's oral agreement with B. A should be bound to the terms of the lease set forth in the attornment certificate.

      3) **Payment of Rent** - A tenant may continue to pay the landlord under a lease agreement until the tenant is notified of an assignment of the lease.

         Example: A leases an apartment from B. B assigns her interest to C. A, who does not know of the assignment, continues to pay rent to B. A's payments to B are a defense in an action by C for rent. Until notified of the assignment, an obligor, like A, may continue to pay the assignor, B.

As between the original landlord and the assignee, the one who holds the interest of the landlord on the date a rental payment is due is entitled to that payment unless the assignment agreement states otherwise.

Example: A owns an apartment building which she sells to B on April 15th. Closing on the building, with assignment of the leases, is scheduled for and held on June 15th. Rent is due from tenants in the building on the first of each month. A is entitled to the rent due June 1st. B is entitled to rent due July 1st.

b. **Transfer of the Tenant's Interest** - A tenant may transfer his or her interest in a lease unless the lease agreement expressly provides otherwise. A transfer of the tenant's interest may be either an *assignment or a sub-lease.*

1) **The Distinction Between an Assignment and a Sub-Lease** - A tenant assigns a lease when the tenant transfers the remainder of the tenant's term. With a sub-lease, the tenant retains a portion of the original lease term after the term of the sub-lease has expired.

Example: A leases Blackacre to B for a term of three years. One year later, B transfers the right of possession to C for a term of one year. The agreement between B and C is a sub-lease because B has the right to possession for a year of the original lease term following the expiration of C's sub-lease. If B had transferred a two-year term to C, the transfer would have been an assignment.

When a sub-lease has taken place the original lease is often called the *head lease.* The original tenant is the *head tenant* and the transferee the *sub-tenant* or *sub-lessee.* The original tenant in an assignment is called the *assignor.* The person acquiring the remainder of the lease term is called the *assignee.*

2) **Liability of the Original Tenant to the Landlord** – Neither an assignment or a sub-lease relieves the original tenant of the tenant's obligations under the original lease, including the obligation to pay rent. Notwithstanding any assignment or sub-lease, the original tenant and the landlord still stand in a contractual relationship with one another the courts call *privity of contract.* They must continue to honor the contractual commitments made in the original lease. If the original tenant is required to pay rent to the landlord accruing during the period a sub-tenant or assignee is in possession, the original tenant is entitled to contribution from the sub-tenant or assignee.

3) **Liability of the Sub-tenant or Assignee to the Landlord** - In the typical case, neither a sub-tenant nor an assignee has entered into a contract with the original landlord. Their agreement is with the original tenant. Therefore, long ago, the common law did not permit the landlord to sue either a sub-tenant or an assignee in contract.

Eventually, however, the courts at common law permitted a landlord to sue on covenants in the original lease that "touched and concerned" the land. This would include the covenant to pay rent. In order to sue on the covenants, however, the landlord had to stand in *privity of estate* with the transferee of the lease. Two persons are in privity of estate when they share successive interests in the land. Thus, landlords stand in privity of estate with assignees but not sub-tenants.

Remember there is a reversion in the head tenant following a sub-lease. The landlord does not come into possession following a sub-lease, but the original tenant does. With an assignment, on the other hand, the original tenant has transferred the remainder of the original lease term. The landlord will come into possession after the assignee's term expires. As a result, at common law, a landlord could sue an assignee on privity of estate for promises that touched and concerned the land like the covenant to pay rent. The landlord could not, however, sue a sub-tenant directly. The sub-tenant does not have privity of estate or contract with the landlord and therefore was not personally liable to the landlord. If a sub-tenant failed to pay rent, a landlord could only sue the head tenant. If the head tenant failed to pay, the landlord could terminate the head lease. That action would end the sub-tenant's right of possession and the sub-tenant could be ejected. The sub-tenant would not, however, be liable for rent to the landlord.

4) **Assumption and Novation Agreements** - Under modern principles of contract law, a sub-tenant may be liable in contract to the landlord as a third party beneficiary. If the sub-tenant expressly agrees in the contract of sub-lease to assume all the obligations of the original lease, many courts would hold that promise was intended to benefit the landlord. The landlord could thus sue the sub-tenant as a third-party beneficiary of that promise. Note there must be express language of assumption in the sub-lease. The courts will not imply an *assumption*.

Similarly, a landlord may expressly agree to release the original tenant from further liability when the original tenant transfers the lease. Such an agreement is called a *novation*. Like assumption agreements, a novation must be expressly agreed to and will not be implied.

IV. RULES AND PROCEDURES DESIGNED TO PROMOTE THE ALIENABILITY OF PROPERTY

Courts and legislatures have developed a number of rules and procedures which have the effect of promoting the alienability of property. These rules and procedures fall into four general categories: (1) rules against restraints on alienation; (2) procedures designed to permit sales of land encumbered by present possessory and future interests where the holders of those interests are at an impasse; (3) rules designed to preserve the value of future interests by regulating waste; and (4) technical rules which free land from contingent future interests.

A. RESTRAINTS ON ALIENATION

The common law disfavored restraints on alienation of legal interests. Restraints are categorized as follows:

1. **Disabling Restraints** - A disabling restraint purports to make a transfer of an interest ineffective. Generally speaking, any disabling restraint on a legal interest is void.

   Example: O leaves his house to his daughter, A for life, with the proviso that the house cannot be sold. The proviso is a disabling restraint on a life estate and is void. The result would be the same if the proviso attempted to deprive A of the right to mortgage the property.

2. **Forfeiture Restraints** - Under a forfeiture restraint the holder of a legal interest loses that interest if they attempt to transfer it. The common law treated forfeiture restraints less harshly than disabling restraints and permitted forfeiture restraints on life estates and future interests. A forfeiture restraint on a fee simple, however, is void.

   Example: O leaves his house to his daughter A for life, with the proviso that if she attempts to sell the house it will pass to O's other daughter, B, for life. The proviso in this variation is a forfeiture restraint on a life estate and might survive judicial scrutiny.

3. **Promissory Restraints** - A legal interest is subject to a promissory restraint when the holder of the interest covenants against transferring it. Again, the common law treated promissory restraints more favorably than disabling restraints. A promissory restraint can be enforced by an award of damages for breach. As a result, the courts have allowed promissory restraints on life estates and interests other than fees. The courts will strike down a promissory restraint on a fee simple.

   Example: O grants Blackacre "to his daughter, A, and her heirs" by a deed in which "A promises on behalf of her heirs, successors, and assigns never to sell Blackacre outside of the family." The restriction is a promissory restraint on a fee simple and would generally be found void. Note that this is a partial restraint. A could sell Blackacre to another member of her family. Nevertheless, the courts at common law would refuse to allow the restraint to impair the alienability of a fee.

4. **Other Permissible Restraints** - Courts have enforced other restraints on alienation in addition to allowing non-disabling restraints on lesser interests than fees.

   The courts, for example, have generally permitted a seller of real property to retain an option to repurchase the land or a right of first refusal if the buyer receives a later offer to purchase the property.

   The courts will also enforce express language in a lease that either prohibits or restricts assignments and sub-leases. The language will be strictly construed, however, because the law looks with disfavor on restraints on alienation.

Example: A leases Blackacre to B pursuant to a written agreement that prohibits sub-leases. Two months later, B assigns her interest to C. A court may hold the assignment did not offend the clause in the original lease. The clause prohibited sub-leases, not assignments.

A common restriction found in leases is one which bans assignments or sub-leases made without the landlord's consent. Traditionally, such clauses were construed to permit the landlord to withhold consent for any reason. Modern cases, particularly with commercial leases, have held the landlord must act in a commercially reasonable manner when the landlord withholds consent. If a tenant's rent is based on gross receipts, a landlord could withhold consent to an assignment if the proposed assignee would be unlikely to generate a comparable level of receipts. A landlord may withhold consent for other commercially sound reasons.

Example: A, an upscale department store, leases space in a mall from B. A's lease prohibits assignments or sub-leases without B' consent. The other tenants in the mall are Gucci, Luis Vuitton, Burberry's, Tiffany's and other high end retailers. A wants to sub-lease to Bargain Basement, Inc. B may withhold consent because the proposed sub-tenant would not suit the tenant mix of the mall.

B. PROCEDURES DESIGNED TO PROTECT HOLDERS OF PRESENT POSSESSORY INTERESTS

If the life tenant and the person or persons holding the remainder following the life estate cannot agree on terms of sale, the property subject to those interests becomes virtually unmarketable. There are few buyers of life estates or lenders willing to take mortgages on life estates. As a result, a life tenant in economic distress can realize little value from the life estate.

1. **Equitable Relief** - The courts of equity could intervene to relieve the economic distress of a life tenant by ordering a sale of the property. The value received could then be equitably allocated between the life tenant and the remaindermen. The courts of equity would entertain such a suit, however, in very limited circumstances. They generally would exercise jurisdiction only if the remainder was held by unascertained persons, such as unborn children. Moreover, they required a showing that the life tenant was suffering hardship and that the interests of the remaindermen could be adequately protected.

2. **Use of a Trust** - Because there is always a potential impasse between the holder of a legal life estate and the holder of the remainder, it is generally unwise to create a legal life estate for a client. A lawyer can avoid the potential impasse through the use of a trust. The trustee holds legal title to the property for the benefit of a life tenant and the remaindermen. The beneficiaries have equitable interests, an equitable life estate and remainder. The trustee, though, holds legal title in fee simple and can therefore dispose of the property in the best interests of the beneficiaries.

C. RULES DESIGNED TO PROTECT THE HOLDERS OF FUTURE INTERESTS

A holder of a future interest in property may find that the holder of the present interest is impairing the value of the property. In these circumstances, the holder of the future interest may find relief under the law of *waste*. The law categorizes waste as follows:

1. **Voluntary Waste** - The holder of a present interest such as a life estate or the tenant of term of years commits *voluntary waste* when he or she commits an act that injures the property. Typical examples would include the destruction of buildings or other improvements to the land, the cutting of trees, or the removal of minerals.

   The following acts are generally *not* considered to be voluntary waste:

   a. **Acts of Maintenance** - The tenant may remove trees or improvements in order to maintain the property. Similarly, natural growth may be removed in the interest of good husbandry.

      Example: A life tenant removes a tree from the front yard of a house because the roots of the tree are threatening the foundation of the building. Such an act will not give rise to an action for waste.

   b. **Acts Permitted By Agreement or the Terms of a Grant** - A lease agreement may permit the tenant to remove minerals or commit acts which would otherwise amount to waste. Similarly, the grantor of a life estate and a remainder may by the terms of the grant permit the life tenant to engage in acts that would otherwise constitute waste. In neither case, will an action for waste lie.

   c. **The Open Mines Doctrine** - The law presumes that an activity that was underway when an estate began may continue without giving rise to liability for waste. Thus, if a mine was open when a life estate began, the life tenant could continue to remove the minerals.

      Example: O owned land from which a logging company harvested timber. O devised a life estate in the land to A with a remainder to B. During the life tenancy, A continued to permit the logging company to remove timber from the land in return for royalties. Although removal of the timber would ordinarily amount to waste, B would probably not have an action against A under the open mines doctrine.

2. **Permissive Waste** - Permissive waste occurs when the tenant in possession neglects to maintain the value of the property. Typical examples would be a failure to keep the premises watertight or a failure to pay charges on the land that were a responsibility of the tenant such as taxes or special assessments.

   a. **Liability Limited to Income of Fair Rental Value** - At common law, a life tenant was not obligated to make repairs to property which cost more than the income generated by the land. Thus, a life tenant is often not liable for catastrophic loss. Similarly, a life tenant was not obligated to pay taxes on the property which exceeded the income derived by the property or its fair rental value.

b. **Liability to Insure Against Loss -** Unless a lease agreement or the terms of a grant provide otherwise, a life tenant or lessee is not required to insure the property against loss.

c. **Liability for Acts of Third Parties** - Generally, a life tenant or lessee is not obligated under the law of waste to repair damage to the property caused by third parties beyond the tenant's control.

3. **Ameliorative Waste** - Acts of waste that actually improve the value of the land are known as *ameliorative waste*. At common law, a life tenant was obligated to maintain property in the condition that existed at the time the tenant took possession. Acts that improved the value of the land, such as demolishing a small structure to build a larger one, could actually give rise to liability for waste. Today, most American jurisdictions do not recognize a cause of action for ameliorative waste.

4. **The Action for Waste** - A court may enjoin voluntary or permissive waste. It may also award money damages to the aggrieved party. An action for waste generally must be brought by the person who holds the vested interest that immediately follows the defendant's.

   Example: O devised Blackacre to A for life, then to B for life, then to C and his heirs. A suffers waste, that is, he permits the property to deteriorate. Under the traditional view, A may be sued for permissive waste by B, but not C. B has the next vested estate. He is in privity with A but C is not.

   Holders of reversions and remainders following life estates and leaseholds are entitled to relief for waste. So are concurrent owners.

   Example: A and B own Blackacre as tenants in common. A announces plans to tear down the manor house on Blackacre. B may enjoin the destruction of the home as a act of voluntary waste.

   Holders of more remote future interests are generally not entitled to bring an action to recover damages for waste. These interests would include contingent remainders and the future interests following defeasible fees. Courts have, however, on occasion enjoined future waste by a person in possession in suits brought by holders of these more remote future interests. A person who has only an expectancy, such as a putative heir, cannot bring an action for waste.

D. RULES THAT CLEAR LAND TITLES OF CONTINGENT FUTURE INTERESTS

The common law developed a number of legal rules that had the effect of clearing land title of contingent future interests. A few of these rules are largely of historical importance although they still surface on bar examinations from time to time! Others remain important.

1. **The Destructibility of Contingent Remainders** - At common law, if a remainder had not vested by the time the preceding estate ended, it was destroyed. The rule cleared titles but has little or no importance today. It is not followed in the United States.

   Example: O grants Blackacre to A for life, then to the first of A's children to come to the bar. A dies, leaving a daughter, B, who is a physician but not a lawyer. At common law, O would own Blackacre in fee simple absolute. The remainder to "the first of A's children to come to the bar" is contingent because it is subject to a condition precedent. That condition had not occurred at the time of A's death. Therefore, the remainder was destroyed and O's reversion would become possessory as a fee simple absolute.

   Today, with the abolition of the doctrine of the destructibility of contingent remainders, O's reversion will still become possessory at A's death. O's fee simple, however, is subject to an executory limitation. If B comes to the bar, she will cut short O's interest. B, therefore, has a springing executory interest.

2. **Merger** - At common law, and still today, if a person holds both a present possessory interest and the next vested future interest, the estates will *merge*.

   Example: O grants a life estate in Blackacre to A with a remainder in fee simple to B. B later sells his interest in Blackacre to A. A's life estate will merge with the vested remainder, leaving A with a fee simple absolute.

   Estates will not merge if there is an intervening vested interest.

   Example: O grants Blackacre "to A for life, then to B for life, then to C and her heirs." C sells her interest in Blackacre to A. A has both a life estate and a vested remainder in fee simple. The interests do not merge, however, because B holds an intervening vested estate, a vested remainder in a life estate.

   At common law, the courts applied the destructibility doctrine to destroy intervening contingent remainders when two vested estates merged. As with the rest of the destructibility doctrine, this rule has little force today.

   Example: O grants Blackacre "to A for life, then to B if he reaches the age of 21, then to C and her heirs." When B is ten years old, A acquires C's remainder. At common law, A's life estate would merge with the vested remainder acquired from C. B's contingent remainder would be destroyed.

3. **Shelley's Case** - The rule in Shelley's case applies if a single instrument conveys a life estate and also purports to convey a remainder to persons identified as the life tenant's heirs. The rule gives the life tenant the remainder and the life estate.

Example: O's last will devises Blackacre "to A for life, then to A's heirs." The Rule in Shelley's case applies. A has both the life estate and the remainder. In this case, because there is no intervening interest, the life estate and remainder will merge leaving A with a fee simple absolute.

The Rule in Shelley's case has been abolished by statute in most jurisdictions. From time to time, however, the rule surfaces in litigation over a will, deed or trust instrument drafted before the effective date of the statute.

4. **Worthier Title** - The doctrine of worthier title applies when a grantor conveys a life estate with a remainder in persons identified as the grantor's heirs. Under the doctrine, the remainder in the grantor's heirs is treated as a reversion in the grantor. In other words, the grantor receives the remainder.

   Example: O conveys Blackacre "to A for life, then to O's heirs." O later drafts a will that takes effect at his death in which he left all his property to his college. O's sole heir is B. Under the doctrine of worthier title, the college will get Blackacre when A dies. The doctrine treats the remainder in O's heirs as O's interest. It will pass through O's will to the college.

The doctrine of worthier title has been abolished in many jurisdictions, particularly with regard to wills. The rule is infrequently applied today as a rule of construction rather than a rule of law. In other words, the effect of the rule can be rebutted with evidence showing the grantor did not intend the rule to apply.

5. **The Rule Against Perpetuities** - John Chipman Gray stated the rule succinctly: "No interest is good unless it must vest, if at all, no later than twenty-one years after some life in being at the creation of the interest." To paraphrase the rule as a positive statement: "A contingent interest is good if you can find some natural person, anyone, of whom you can say that within that person's lifetime plus twenty-one years, the interest will necessarily either vest or fail to vest."

Watch Out!

How to apply the Rule Against Perpetuities:
If there is ***any possibility***, no matter how unlikely, that a non-reversionary future interest might **vest** (i.e. give an immediate, fixed right of present or future enjoyment) more than 21 years after the death of all the **lives in being** (i.e. anyone who has been conceived by the time of the grant, preferably someone named in the grant) at the time of the creation of the interest, then the property interest is void (i.e. it is treated as if it never existed).

a. **Interests Subject to the Rule** - The rule *applies to* a broad array of contingent interests in real property: contingent remainders; executory interests; vested remainders that are subject to open; and in many states, options to purchase property and repurchase. The rule also applies to powers of appointment under a will.

The rule *does not apply to*: reversions, possibilities of reverter; and rights of entry even though they may not become possessory until well after the period of the rule.

> **Watch Out!**
>
> To avoid common Rule Against Perpetuities testing traps, you must remember that the Rule Against Perpetuities does **not** apply in every situation. The bar examiners will try to trick you into making an interest void on the basis that it violates the Rule Against Perpetuities when it is not even subject to the Rule Against Perpetuities. To avoid this trap, it is helpful to remember what types of interests are NOT subject to the Rule Against Perpetuities.
>
> The following interests are **NOT** subject to the Rule Against Perpetuities:
>
> - **Interests held by grantor**
>   (such as reversion, possibility of reverter, right of entry); and
> - **Vested interests**
>   (other than vested remainders subject to open).

Example: O donates property "to the Blackacre School District for so long as the property is used for school purposes." O retains a possibility of reverter that may not become possessory until well beyond twenty-one years after O and everyone else living at the time of the gift has died. Nevertheless, the rule does not apply to interests retained by a grantor, like O's possibility of reverter.

> **Watch Out!**
>
> Watch out for provisions that require title to pass to a third party if the property is no longer being used for certain specified purposes. It is impossible to predict when such usage will come to an end. Therefore, any such provision would violate the Rule Against Perpetuities, because there is a possibility the subsequent interest in the property may vest outside the period of the Rule.

Example: Suppose O had donated the property "to the Blackacre School District for so long as the property is used for school purposes, and if it should ever cease to be so used, to A and her heirs." The rule now applies. A's future interest is an executory interest. It may not vest within the period of the rule and is therefore invalid.

There are other exceptions to the rule. States that apply the rule to options to purchase land, generally do not apply it to options held by a tenant under a lease. Similarly, someone who owns a subsurface estate, such as mineral rights in coal, can have a purchase option of unlimited duration to purchase the surface. The rule also does not apply to gifts to a charity with a gift over to another charity.

Example: O donates property "to the Blackacre Home for Wayward Children for so long as the property is used as a children's home, and should it ever ceased to be so used, to the Blackacre Nursing Home." Under the exception applicable to charities, the executory interest in the Blackacre Nursing Home will survive the rule.

> **Watch Out!**
>
> Remember that when the Rule Against Perpetuities is violated, the entire transaction is not voided, only the offending part of it fails. Be sure that you know what happens to the future interest after the Rule Against Perpetuities is violated. The question may not end with the answer that the rule has been violated. The bar examiners may take it a step further and ask you to determine who ends up with the property.

b. **Period of the Rule** - The period of the Rule begins to run at the time of the creation of the interest subject to the Rule. Remember an interest conveyed by deed takes effect upon delivery. An interest devised in a will takes effect at the testator's death. An interest conveyed in trust takes effect for purpose of the Rule when trust becomes irrevocable.

The period of the rule then runs for the lifetime of a person, often referred to as the measuring life, plus twenty-one years.

c. **The Measuring Life** - Any person, or class of persons if the class is not unreasonably large, can be used to mark the period of the rule. Use the person who can affect the vesting of the interest as the measuring life. For example, if an interest is contingent on someone doing something, use the someone as the measuring life.

Example: Consider a grant "to A for life, remainder to B if she comes to the bar." B has a contingent remainder. The remainder will vest in interest when she is admitted to the bar. Use B as the measuring life. B will either be admitted to the bar or fail to be admitted to the bar within her lifetime plus twenty-one years. Her contingent reminder, therefore, is valid.
If an interest is contingent because it is given to an open class, use the life of the person whose death will result in the closing of the class. For example, if an interest is in a class identified as "A's children," use A as the measuring life. A cannot have children after his death. (A life in any stage of gestation is considered a life in being for purposes of the Rule Against Perpetuities).

Example: O grants Blackacre "to A for life, then to B for life, then to A's children and their heirs." In this grant, A's children have a contingent remainder. They are unascertained persons. We will know, however, who A's children are within twenty-one years of his death. Use A, therefore, as a measuring life. The remainder is good. Note that in this example, you would have to go through the same analysis even if A had a child at the time of the grant. That child would have a vested remainder but the remainder would be subject to open. Remember the rule applies to remainders that are subject to open.

Look out for an interest given to an open class which has a contingency based on age longer than twenty-one years. The rule is almost certainly violated.

Example: O devises Blackacre, "to his children for their lives, and then to his grandchildren who reach the age of thirty." There are two class gifts in this example. The remainder given to O's children is closed because O is dead. This is a devise. There can, however, be more grandchildren as long as the children are alive. Therefore, the class gift to the grandchildren is subject to open and will fail under the rule. A grandchild born after the devise might be the first grandchild to reach the age of thirty. Therefore, the remainder would vest outside the period of the rule, a life in being at the time of the creation of the interest, plus twenty-one years.

As the last example illustrates, beware if the measuring life (i.e, the person who can affect vesting of the interest) is not a life in being at the time of the creation of the interest. The rule is almost certainly violated.

Example: Consider a grant "to A for life, then to the first of A's children to come to the bar." A is alive at the time of the grant and has two children B and C. The first child of A to come to the bar may be a person not yet born and therefore the contingent remainder fails under the rule. To illustrate, suppose A has another child, D, two years after the grant. A then dies. B and C die, as does everyone else living at the time of the grant. Twenty-two years later, D is admitted to the bar. The remainder could vest outside the period of the Rule and is void.

d. **Remorseless Logic** - The Rule Against Perpetuities as applied by the courts of common law was remorseless. If an interest offended the rule it was stricken out, rendered null and void. At the same time, the common law courts approached the rule as a test rule of logical proof and not necessarily one calling for common sense. The courts did not try to save contingent interests. They would strike them under the rule if there was any possibility, however unlikely, that they would vest outside the period of the rule. Generations of law students have given colorful names to most notorious examples:

The Fertile Octogenarian - Assume A is eighty-five years old at the time she is granted Blackacre for life, remainder to her children for life with a remainder to her grandchildren in fee simple. The common law courts found the rule to be violated on the unlikely assumption that A could have another child born after the grant. The gift to the grandchildren would be stricken, leaving the grantor with a reversion that would become possessory when A's last child died.

The Slothful Executor - O's will leaves Blackacre to A after settlement of O's estate. A's springing executory interest was struck down because it was theoretically possible, though very unlikely, that O's estate might not be settled within the period of the rule. Blackacre would pass through the residuary clause of O's will or by intestate succession if O's will did not have such a clause.

The Unborn Widow (or Widower) - Consider a conveyance to A for life, then A's widow for life, then to A's surviving children. In this conveyance, the children must survive the widow for their remainder to vest. Because A might marry someone not yet born at the time of the conveyance, the remainder might vest outside the period of the rule. It would be stricken leaving A with a life estate, A's widow with a contingent remainder in a life estate and the grantor with a reversion in fee simple absolute. The contingent remainder in A's widow is good under the rule because you can use A as a measuring life. We will know who the widow is at A's death.

Watch Out!

If you are having difficulty determining whether or not an interest is valid under the Rule Against Perpetuities, try to come up with a scenario that will **not** satisfy the Rule. If you can think of any situation, no matter how unlikely, in which an interest may vest *after* the perpetuities period ends, the Rule has been violated and the interest is void. The Rule requires that the interest must vest within the perpetuities period in order to be valid, not just that it may do so.

e. **Reform of the Rule** - Statutes have reformed the rule against perpetuities in a majority of states. These reforms vary from abolition of the rule to simply legislating against its most peculiar applications like the notorious examples listed above.

Many states have adopted a "wait and see" approach to determine whether a contingent interest will vest or fail to vest within the period of the rule. Under this approach, a court tests whether a contingent interest vests or not outside the period by actual rather than possible events.

The Uniform Statutory Rule Against Perpetuities adopts the wait and see approach and amends the period to 90 years, as opposed to the common law "life in being plus twenty-one years."

Example: Consider once again a grant "to A for life, then to the first of A's children to come to the bar." In a jurisdiction that has adopted the Uniform Statutory Rule Against Perpetuities, you would wait and see whether A's first child to pass the bar did so within 90 years of the effective date of the grant. You would not automatically invalidate the contingent remainder because it might vest too remotely.

V. CONCURRENT INTERESTS

Property can be owned by two or more persons at the same time. There are three types of concurrent estates recognized at common law that are still widely recognized today: *tenancies in common; joint tenancies;* and *tenancies by the entirety.*

A. THE TENANCY IN COMMON

A tenancy in common arises when two or more persons own property with a simultaneous right to possession.

1. **Attributes** - Each tenant in common has a right to use and enjoy the entire property, a relation the common law labeled "unity of possession." Tenants in common may acquire their interests at different times and may own unequal shares:

   Example: A owns Blackacre in fee simple absolute. He sells a two-thirds interest in Blackacre to B. As a result, A and B own Blackacre as tenants in common with B holding two-thirds interest, and A, one-third. Both have an undivided right to possession of the whole but if they sell the property for $30,000, B will receive $20,000 and A, $10,000.

   Tenants in common may sell, lease or otherwise transfer their interests. The interest of a tenant in common is also devisable and inheritable. There is no right of survivorship in the relation:

   Example: A and B own Blackacre as tenants in common when A dies intestate, leaving C as her sole heir at law. As a result, B and C now own Blackacre as tenants in common.

2. **Creation** - Today, the law presumes a tenancy in common is created anytime a devise or conveyance is made to two or more persons to enjoy at the same time.

B. JOINT TENANCY

A ***joint tenancy*** is a concurrent estate where the tenants have a right of survivorship, meaning that when one tenant dies, the remaining tenants succeed to the decedent's interest.

1. **Attributes** - The common law required joint tenants to share "four unities:"

   a. ***Unity of Time*** - the joint tenants must have acquired their interests at the same time;

   b. ***Unity of Title*** - the joint tenants must have acquired their title through the same deed, will or other instrument;

   c. ***Unity of Interest*** - the joint tenants must have held equal shares; and

   d. ***Unity of Possession*** - each joint tenants must have a right to possession of the whole, the only unity required of a tenancy in common.

2. **Creation** - A joint tenancy arose at common law anytime a concurrent estate was created with the four unities. Today, a joint tenancy usually can only be created by specifically mentioning the right of survivorship. Remember the law presumes a tenancy in common today.

   Example: O's will devises his house to his two children A and B. Although A and B acquire the house at the same time, by the same instrument, in equal shares, with the same right to possess the whole, they would be tenants in common under the modern presumption. O's will would have to specify that A and B enjoy a right of survivorship in order to create a joint or survivorship tenancy. An unambiguous devise would read "to A and B as joint tenants with right of survivorship, and not as tenants in common."

3. **Severance** - At common law, a joint tenant could sever the unities of time and title by conveying their interest to a third party. The third party would then stand as a tenant in common with the remaining joint tenants. As a result, the right of survivorship in the tenant's share who conveyed their interest would be destroyed. This ability of a joint tenant to unilaterally *sever* a joint tenancy by an *inter vivos* conveyance remains a feature of the law today.

   Example: A, B, and C own Blackacre as joint tenants with right of survivorship. C conveys her interest to D. A then dies intestate leaving E as his sole heir. Then C dies leaving a will that named F as her sole beneficiary of her estate. Blackacre is owned by B and D as tenants in common with B holding a two thirds share. When C conveyed to D, she severed her joint tenancy with A and B. They no longer enjoyed a right of survivorship in her share, so C's death did not effect their interest. D owns C's share by virtue of the conveyance. A and B, however, remained joint tenants between themselves after C conveyed her share to D. When A died, therefore, his share passed by right of survivorship to B. Nothing passed by intestate succession to E.

   a. A Mortgage by One Joint Tenant - At common law a borrower conveyed title to a mortgage lender in order to secure a mortgage loan. As a result, if the borrower was a joint tenant, a mortgage severed the relation. Today, most states treat a mortgage as a lien on property with title remaining in the borrower. As a result, in "lien theory" states, a joint tenant may obtain a mortgage on their share of a property without severing the joint tenancy. If the remaining joint tenants survive the mortgagor some states hold the mortgage lien does not survive. The property passes by right of survivorship to the remaining tenants free of the mortgage lien.

   b. A Lease by One Joint Tenant - At common law, a lease by one joint tenant severed the joint tenancy because the unities of possession and title were destroyed. The lessee enjoyed the right of possession formerly enjoyed by the lessor. The joint tenant who leased the property held title subject to the lease while the remaining joint tenants did not. If the lessor died before the other joint tenants, the lessee would stand as a tenant in common for the remainder of the lease term with the survivors.

A few American courts have held that a lease does not sever a joint tenancy. As a result, they have permitted the joint tenants who survive the joint tenant who leased the property to evict the lessee. See, ***Tenhet v. Boswell,*** 18 Cal. 3d 150 (1976).

C. TENANCY BY THE ENTIRETIES

A *tenancy by the entirety* is a concurrent estate that shares most of the features of a joint tenancy but adds a fifth unity, the unity of marriage.

1. **Attributes** - Tenants by the entirety enjoy a right of survivorship. Title to property held by the entireties will pass at death to the surviving spouse. The feature that distinguishes a tenancy by the entirety from a joint tenancy is that, in most states that recognize the estate, neither the husband nor the wife can unilaterally sever a tenancy by the entirety. One spouse alone cannot convey any interest in property held by the entireties, nor can the separate creditors of either spouse reach the property.

   The Supreme Court of the United States, however, has recently held that a federal tax lien will attach to the separate interest of a spouse who holds property by the entirety." ***United States v. Craft,*** No. 00-1831 (U.S. Apr. 17, 2002).

2. **Creation** - In the twenty or so states that recognize tenants by the entireties, the estate arises when property is conveyed to a husband and wife unless the terms of the conveyance state otherwise.

3. **Severance** - In most states that recognize the estate, a tenancy by the entirety cannot be unilaterally severed by either spouse and will end only upon:

   a. **a release** - consent by one tenant by the entirety to a conveyance by the other;

   b. **mutual agreement** - where both spouses join in a conveyance, mortgage or other disposition; or

   c. **divorce** - a final divorce decree converts a tenancy by the entirety into a tenancy in common unless the property settlement reached in the divorce proceeding provides otherwise.

D. RIGHTS OF CONCURRENT OWNERS *INTER SE*

A co-tenant in any of the concurrent estates has rights and duties with respect to the other co-tenants.

1. **Ouster** - Regardless of the form of concurrent estate, each co-tenant has a right to the possession of the entire property. When one co-tenant denies possession to another, the law calls the denial an *ouster.* The excluded tenant can bring an action in ejectment to recover possession. The excluded tenant can also bring an action to recover money damages for *mesne profits*, the fair rental value of the property.

2. **Rent** - In the majority of states, a co-tenant in possession is not obligated to pay rent to the other co-tenants absent an ouster. However, if a third party, someone other than a co-tenant, is in possession of property held as a concurrent estate, all the co-tenants are entitled to share in any rent received from that third party.

3. **Profits** - A co-tenant who derives profits from the land in the form of minerals, timber, oil and gas, generally must account to the other co-tenants for their respective share of the profits.

4. **Taxes and Mortgage Payments** - A co-tenant who pays more than his or her share of taxes, mortgage payments, special assessments or other carrying charges on the land, has a right of contribution from the other co-tenants.

5. **Repairs and Improvements** - By contrast, a co-tenant who incurs expenses repairing or improving the property generally has no right of contribution from the other co-tenants. A co-tenant may however receive credit for reasonable repairs in an accounting or partition action. As for expenses incurred for improvements, the court will generally allow a credit for these expenses in an accounting or partition action if the improvements increased the value of the property.

E. PARTITION ACTIONS

Co-tenants can petition a court to *partition* property held as a concurrent estate. In a partition action, two kinds of relief are generally available:

1. **Partition in Kind** - A court may physically divide property held in a concurrent estate and award each co-tenant a portion of the property as sole owner. Such relief is known as a *partition in kind.* If a portion of the property awarded to one co-tenant is more valuable than another, the court may order the co-tenant receiving the more valuable parcel to compensate the remaining tenants. The sum paid to compensate the other tenants is called an *owelty.*

2. **Partition by Sale** - A court may order a partition by sale if a partition in kind is impractical. The sales proceeds are then distributed among the co-tenants. In distributing the sales proceeds, the court may allow credits to co-tenants who have claims against the other tenants.

3. **Amicable Partition** - If all the persons with an interest in a concurrent estate agree on a manner of physically dividing the property, they can file an uncontested amicable partition action to have their agreement made a matter of record. Naturally, if all the co-tenants agree, they can join in a sale to a third party and divide the proceeds among themselves.

F. MARITAL ESTATES

Marriage affects the property rights of the spouses. Several states still recognize common law dower and most states have enacted an elective share statute.

1. **Dower** - At common law, a wife acquired upon the death of her husband a life estate in

all the inheritable real property the husband owned at any time during their marriage. This right was known as *dower*. Most states have abolished dower but where it still exists it is made available to both husbands and wives. In those states, a buyer, mortgagee or other transferee of property from one of the spouses, takes their interest subject to the other's dower rights unless the other spouse has released those rights. A divorce decree terminates dower rights.

Example: A owned two properties when he married B. He owned Blackacre in fee simple as a joint tenant with his sister. He was the sole owner of Greenacre. Without B's consent, A sold his interest in Greenacre to C. A later died. B's dower rights attached to Greenacre but not Blackacre. A's interest in Blackacre as a joint tenant passed by right of survivorship to his sister. Because A's interest was thus not inheritable, dower never attached to it. Dower did attach to Greenacre, however. C, therefore, acquired Greenacre subject to B's dower rights and B is entitled to a one-third interest for life in the estate.

2. **Elective Share** – Under modern statutes of descent and distribution surviving spouses are entitled to a share of decedent's intestate estate. If the decedent has died testate, leaving a will that gives less than the intestate share to the surviving spouse, the survivor can elect to take the intestate share in lieu of what he or she would receive under the will. The elective share is generally determined by reference to the decedent's probate estate and is not available for assets that pass outside probate.

Example: A dies, leaving a will that bequeaths $100 to her husband and $100 to the American Red Cross. Before she died A had a life estate in Blackacre with a remainder in her daughter. A also held a $1 million brokerage account as a joint tenant with right of survivorship in her daughter. She also had a $100,000 life insurance policy that named her daughter as loss payee. A's husband does not have a claim against A's estate under the elective share statute. The husband received one half the probate estate. A's remaining assets passed outside her estate.

VI. NON-POSSESSORY INTERESTS

The law recognizes interests in real property that do not involve possession of the land. These interests include *easements*, *profits*, *real covenants*, *equitable servitudes* and *licenses*.

A. EASEMENTS, PROFITS AND LICENSES

Easements, profits and licenses are rights to use the land of another in a manner that would otherwise be a trespass. They are almost always *affirmative* interests, rights of use, rather than *negative* interests, rights to restrict another's use.

1. **Easements** - An *easement* is an interest in land that gives the holder of the easement the right to use the land of another for some limited purpose. Common easements involve the right to drive over another's land or the right to lay utility or rail lines under or over another's land.

2. **Classification** - Easements are classified as appurtenant or in gross. They are also said to be affirmative or negative.

   a. **Appurtenant Easements** - Rights to an easement may be tied to a parcel of land. In such a case, the easement is said to be *appurtenant.* The parcel of land benefitted by the easement is called the *dominant* estate or tenement. The land burdened by the easement is called the *servient* estate or tenement . Appurtenant easements pass with title to the dominant estate. The law presumes easements are appurtenant absent clear evidence to the contrary.

      Example: A conveys Blackacre to B. The deed to Blackacre contains a grant of an easement entitling B to use the drive over a neighboring parcel, Whiteacre. Two months later B sells Blackacre to C. The easement in this example is appurtenant. Blackacre is the dominant estate. Whiteacre is the servient tenement. C will enjoy the same right to use the drive that B did.

   b. **Easements In Gross** - An easement *in gross* is personal in the sense that it does not benefit a parcel of land but rather, a particular person. The rights of utility companies and railroads to their lines are generally easements in gross.

      Because the benefit of an easement *in gross* is not tied to land it does not pass with any particular parcel. At common law, easements in gross were considered truly personal and consequently, the courts did not permit them to be transferred or devised. Today, any commercial easement is freely transferable as is any other easement where the parties have expressed an intention that be assignable.

      Example: A farmer, A, granted B the right to hunt and fish on A's land during season. B attempted to sell his rights to C. A could block C from hunting and fishing on his land. Even if the right A gave B was construed as an easement and not a revocable license, the easement was in gross. In this case, A did not intend the right to be assignable, and it is not commercial. As such, a court would likely hold that it was not assignable.

3. **Affirmative Easements** - The vast majority of easements are *affirmative*, in the sense that they involve the right to use another's land in a particular way. The right to use another's land for ingress and egress is affirmative. The right to lay cable television or electrical lines is also affirmative.

4. **Negative Easements** - Negative easements are rare. They involve a right to restrict another's use of their land. The English courts limited negative easements to four types:

   a. ***Light*** - The holder of easement of light can prevent the owner of the burdened land from blocking light shining on the holder's land;

   b. ***Air*** - The holder of an easement of air can prevent the owner of another parcel from restricting the holder's flow of air;

c. ***Support*** - The holder of a support easement can prevent a neighbor from undermining a building on the holder's land; and

d. ***Preservation of a Watercourse*** - The holder of this negative easement can prevent another from interfering with an artificial stream or watercourse running through the holder's land.

American courts have not been as restrictive as the English courts in recognizing negative easements. For example, the American courts have recognized negative easements designed to preserve a scenic view. In recent years, many states have enacted statutes recognizing negative conservation easements.

5. **Creation** - Easements can be created by express grant or estoppel. They can also arise by implication or operation of law.

a. **Express Easements** - Easements are an interest in real property. As such, the grant of an easement must comply with the statute of frauds. Usually, this will entail a written grant or deed signed by the holder of the servient estate. It is good practice to use language of grant describing the interest as an easement and to carefully delineate its use. Otherwise, ambiguities can arise.

Example: A signed a written deed which granted and conveyed a "right of way" to B and his heirs. The deed described the right of way by metes and bounds. Arguably, this deed gives B a fee simple in the strip of land described rather than an easement.

An express easement may be created by the grantor reserving or excepting an easement across land the grantor is conveying in fee simple to another. At common law, a grantor could not reserve an easement in favor of a third party, however. The grantor was required to reserve the easement and then grant it, in a second transaction, to the third party. Modern cases have declined to follow this rule and have permitted reservation of an easement in a third party.

Example: A conveyed a lot to B reserving a right in favor of A's church to use the lot for Sunday parking. Under the older view, the reservation of the easement in A's church would be invalid. The modern view would allow A to reserve the easement in favor of her church. *See,* ***Willard v. First Church of Christ Scientist,*** 498 P.2d 987 (Calif. 1972).

b. **Easements by Estoppel** - An easement may arise by estoppel. A landowner who permits another to rely upon a supposed easement may be estopped to deny the easement use insofar as it is necessary to prevent injustice.

Example: A, the owner of Blackacre, permits B, the owner of neighboring land to use a road that crosses Blackacre. A, however, puts nothing in writing and under the statute of frauds, B has no more than license to cross Blackacre. B, however, in reliance on the continued right to use the road, builds a house on a portion of his land reached by the road. A then attempts to block B's access to the road. A should be estopped from denying B's use of the road. B relied on continued use of the road in undertaking the expense of building the house.

Easements by estoppel may also arise when a real estate developer shows prospective purchasers of lots in a proposed sub-division maps or plats that mark access roads and the like.

c. **Implied Easements** - In some circumstances, the courts will imply an easement when an owner of a tract of land divides it and conveys away part without providing for an easement.

Courts are somewhat more willing to imply a grant of an easement than a reservation of an easement. With a reservation, the grantor is retaining the land benefited by the easement and a more searching inquiry may be called for because the grantor could have provided for the easement in the deed. The courts have fewer misgivings with an implied grant which involves construing the deed against the grantor. An implied grant of an easement benefits the grantee of the divided parcel.

1. **Easements Implied By Necessity** - The courts will imply an easement by necessity if what was once a single tract is divided creating a parcel that has no ready access except over other land. The courts insist on a showing that an easement implied by necessity is, indeed, *strictly necessary*. While this does not mean a total lack of access for the locked parcel, it does mean there is no alternative to the implied easement that can be obtained at reasonable expense.

   An easement by necessity will not be implied without a showing of two elements: a *prior unity of ownership* and *strict necessity*.

   Example: A owns Blackacre, a square tract of land of approximately two acres. Blackacre can be reached over a paved road on its south side. A conveys the northern half of Blackacre to B in a deed that fails to provide for an easement. A court could imply an easement of necessity in favor of B's land running over the southern lot retained by A. There was once unity of ownership in the two parcels. The lot conveyed to B has no alternative access except over A's land.

2. **Easements Implied from a Pre-Existing Use** - Courts will imply an easement without a showing of strict necessity if the land was used in a manner consistent with the implied easement before it was divided.

   Three elements must exist to imply an easement from a pre-existing use: a ***prior unity of ownership***; a ***prior use of the land*** in the fashion called for by the implied easement; and a ***showing of reasonable, not strict, necessity.***

Example: A owns Blackacre, a square two-acre tract bounded on the north by Northern Avenue and on the south by South Street. A builds a house on the northern half of Blackacre. She uses a driveway to reach the house that crosses the southern half of Blackacre and connect to South Street. A divides Blackacre and sells the house and northern half of the parcel to B. B's deed did not mention an easement. A court could imply an easement that would permit B to continue to use the driveway. There was prior unity of ownership, the drive was in use before the division of the land and it is necessary. Note B could build a new drive to Northern Avenue but should not be required to do so. A showing of reasonable necessity, not strict necessity, will support a finding of an easement implied from a pre-existing use. Note: this is an implied grant. The easement will burden A's, the grantor's, land and therefore the courts are somewhat more willing to imply it.

The pre-existing use of the easement is sometimes called a *quasi-easement.* Courts that use the term often speak of implying an easement from a quasi-easement.

3. **Easements Arising By Prescription** - An easement can be acquired by operation of law as a result of long, continuous use. Such an easement is called an *easement by prescription.*

Prescription is the *actual*, *adverse*, *exclusive*, *open, notorious* and *continuous* use of another's land throughout the period established by the statute of limitations on the owner's cause of action against the user.

a. **An Actual, Open and Notorious Use** - A person claiming an easement by prescription must in fact use the land of another in a manner that gives notice to the landowner. An adverse use undertaken above or on the surface of the land usually meets this requirement. Underground easements for drains, pipes or sewers often do not. If a utility service is provided to a house, however, the homeowner may be charged with notice of an underground utility line.

b. **Adverse Use** - The use must be adverse or hostile to the interest of the owner of the servient estate. If the owner of the servient estate has permitted a use, it will rarely rise to a prescriptive right. Because the use must give rise to a cause of action in the owner of the servient estate, American law does not recognize negative easements by prescription such as the English doctrine of *ancient lights.*

Example: For decades, A and B have owned neighboring lots on which each built a ranch house. B tears down his ranch house and builds a three-story home. The new structure blocks the light that previously entered A's living room through a picture window. A has no cause of action against B under American law. A could not acquire a negative easement of light by prescription because during the decades B lived in a ranch house on his lot, A had no cause of action against him as he would if B were engaged in an adverse affirmative use. Under English law, A could claim under the doctrine of ancient lights to have acquired a negative easement by prescription to the light that once entered his picture window.

c. **Exclusivity** - The adverse use must be one that is not shared with the public. Exclusivity means something somewhat different than it does in adverse possession cases. A person may acquire an easement by prescription without physically excluding the owner of the servient estate.

Example: A and B own neighboring parcels. B uses a drive across A' s land that A uses as well. If all the other elements for acquiring an easement by prescription are met, B may acquire a prescriptive easement to continue to use the drive. His use is exclusive in the sense that he has used the land in a manner not shared by the general public.

Generally, the exclusivity requirement prevents the public from acquiring rights by prescription. If the public has long used private land, however, some courts will hold the owner made an *implied dedication* of that land to the public. Long acquiescence by the owner in the public's use may be treated as indicative of the owner's intent to dedicate the land to public use.

Example: A owns land adjacent to a public beach. Sunbathers routinely cross A's land to reach the beach. If A does not block public access to his land and the use of the public long continues, A may be held to have dedicated to public use that portion of his land used by the sunbathers.

d. **Continuous Use** - A use must continue for the relevant period of limitations in order to result in an easement by prescription. At common law, the period was twenty years. The continuity requirement does not mean a person must use an easement every day. If a person uses the servient estate with the frequency that is normal for the kind of easement claimed, a prescriptive right may result.

Example: Each Fall, A used a dirt road over B's land to bring his harvesting machinery to a corner of A's farmland. B attempts to block A from using the road. A would have a claim that he acquired a prescriptive right to use the road each harvesting season.

Prescription is very similar to adverse possession, which is discussed, *infra.* Issues like the tolling of statutes of limitation and tacking would be treated in the same fashion if they arose in a dispute over a prescriptive easement or in a case involving a claim of adverse possession.

6. **Scope of Easements** - The holder of an easement cannot enlarge its scope in a manner that would unduly increase the burden of the easement on the servient estate. The increased burden may be enjoined or may support an award of money damages for trespass. A court may find an actionable, undue burden if the holder of an easement alters its use, attempts to relocate it or increases the size or nature of the dominant estate.

   a. **Use** - The use of an easement is limited to its original scope. With express easements, courts will look to the term of the instrument creating the easement to determine its scope. With easements created by estoppel, pre-existing use or prescription, the courts will determine the scope from the manner in which the servient estate was used before the courts determined the use gave rise to an easement. With easements by necessity, the courts attempt to limit the scope of the implied easement to extent of the necessity.

      Example: A granted B the right to lay underground television cable across A' s yard. B proposes to lay a sewer line across the line of the easement. A can enjoin B from laying the sewer line. The action would enlarge the use of the easement beyond its original scope.

      Not every change in the use of an easement is actionable. Courts permit changes in use that reflect advances in technology that do not unduly increase the burden on the servient estate. Thus, roadways once used by a neighbor's horse and carriage could be later used by the neighbor's automobile. In recent years, courts have permitted telephone companies to lay television cable over their easements without finding a actionable overburdening of the servient estate.

   b. **Location and Size** - The holder of an easement cannot relocate it even if the action seems reasonable under the circumstances. The holder of the servient tenement cannot relocate it either. The same rule applies if either attempts to enlarge or diminish the size of the easement. Generally, the parties need to reach a mutually satisfactory agreement to relocate or resize an easement.

   c. **Enlargement of the Dominant Estate** - The holder of an easement appurtenant cannot enlarge the dominant estate.

      Example: A owns a lot which reaches a road by way of an easement over B's farm. A later acquires another lot next to her own. A cannot use the easement over B's farm to reach her new lot.

      Courts may also find that a major change in the use of the dominant estate impermissibly enlarges the scope of an easement.

      Example: A owns a house that reaches a road by way of an easement over B's land. A proposes to convert the house into a retail store. The change from a residential to a commercial use of the dominant estate would likely support a finding that A overburdened B's land. The frequency of use of A's easement is likely to increase.

7. **Termination of Easements** - Easements can come to an end in a number of ways which include:

   a. **The Easement's Own Terms** - An express easement may have a termination date or it may be defeasible upon the happening of a stated event. For example, a person may permit parking on her land for so long as a neighboring parcel is used as a church. If an easement has a stated purpose, the implication arises that the easement will end when the purpose is served:

      Example: A acquired an easement over B's land for the express purpose of a road to truck minerals extracted from A's mine. A court could hold the easement terminated when the mine was exhausted.

   b. **The Law's Purpose In Establishing the Easement Is Served** – Implied easements end when the law's purpose has been served. Thus, an easement implied by necessity ends when the necessity has ended. An easement arising by estoppel may terminate when justice no longer requires recognition of the easement.

      Example: A gives B oral permission to use a road over A's land. B builds a house on her land in reliance on A's assurance that she can use the road. As noted above, the courts would likely find an easement by estoppel has been created by B's detrimental reliance. Assume, however, that B's house is later destroyed by fire. Some authorities hold that justice no longer requires recognition of the easement. There is no longer a need to protect B's reliance interest.

   c. **A Release** - The holder of an easement can bring it to an end by a written release. Remember an easement is an interest in real property subject to the statute of frauds. A release must generally be in writing signed by the holder of the right of use.

   d. **Merger** - If a person acquires both the dominant and servient estates an appurtenant easement will terminate. The easement merges into the larger, possessory estate.

   e. **Destruction of the Servient Tenement** - In some cases, an easement will end with the destruction of the servient tenement.

      Example: A coffee shop has an easement which permits the shop to sell coffee and donuts at a kiosk located in the lobby of an office building. The building is destroyed by a fire. A court would likely rule the coffee shop's easement terminated.

   f. **Prescription or Adverse Possession** - A person can lose an easement through prescription or adverse possession if someone uses an easement or takes possession of the servient estate adversely for the requisite length of time.

g. **Abandonment** - A holder of an easement may abandon it just as a person may abandon any other property interest. Remember mere non-use does not amount to abandonment. The holder of the easement must manifest an unequivocal intention to give up the easement in addition to forgoing its use for an extended period of time.

h. **Other Causes** - In general easements can come to an end for the same reasons any other interest in property terminates. An easement can be taken in eminent domain. A good faith purchaser may have acquired the servient estate without notice of the easement and so on.

8. **Profits** - A *profit á prendre,* or more simply, a *profit*, is a non-possessory right to remove some product from another's land. For example, the right to take timber, minerals, water, fish or game from another's land might all be established through the grant of a profit.

   The law governing easements largely governs profits with few exceptions. All profits are affirmative for example. They will not be implied by necessity or pre-existing use.

9. **Licenses** - A license is a personal privilege to use the land of another in a manner that would otherwise give rise to a cause of action for trespass.

   a. **Creation** - The law treats a license differently than an easement or profit in that a license is not generally considered an interest in real property. As such it can be created without compliance with the statute of frauds. Any competent evidence that the licensor has conferred a right on the licensee will suffice to create a license. Typical examples of licenses are the rights one acquires upon purchasing a ticket to a movie, concert or ball game.

   b. **Revocation** - Generally, a license is revocable at the will of the licensor. There is a limited exception to this rule, however, for a license coupled with an interest. If a licensee holds personal property on the licensor's land, the licensee has the right to remove the property.

   Example: A leases a bar and grill. He gives a vending machine company the right to place and maintain a jukebox in the bar. A did not put anything in writing. He also did not state how long the company could keep the machine in the leasehold. The company enjoys a license coupled with an interest. The lessee of the bar, A, can revoke the license at anytime but he must allow the vending machine company a reasonable time to remove the jukebox.

B. REAL COVENANTS AND EQUITABLE SERVITUDES

The law enforces promises intended to preserve or enhance the value of land. Typical examples would include promises or covenants that require property owners in a subdivision to build houses set back an agreed distance from the street. Other covenants may restrict use of the houses to single family dwellings or provide minimum lot sizes. The law of contracts is perfectly adequate to enforce such promises between the original parties to the covenant. The promises would not be very useful in preserving the value of the land, however, if they were not binding on the contracting parties' successors in interest to the land. The law of real covenants and equitable servitudes provides a means of enforcing such promises on subsequent owners of the land. If a party seeks to enforce such a promise at law, that is through an award of money damages, we call the promise a *real covenant*. It is more common to seek equitable enforcement of the promise through injunctive relief. In proceeding for an injunction, the promise is called an *equitable servitude*.

1. **Real Covenants** - To enforce a covenant through an award of money damages, the law traditionally required: (1) an enforceable contract; (2) made by the parties with the intent to bind their successors; (3) with a promise that "touched and concerned" the land; and (4) with a relationship between the contracting parties and their successors the law called "horizontal" and "vertical privity." In addition to these traditional elements from English law, all American jurisdictions have adopted recording statutes and legislation protecting good faith purchasers who do not have notice of a prior property interest. While the discussion that follows focuses on the traditional elements, remember a good faith purchaser without notice of a covenant may take free of its restrictions.

   a. **An Enforceable Contract** - A real covenant begins its legal life as a contract. If a promise is unenforceable as a contract it generally cannot be enforced as a real covenant. Real covenants must comply with the statute of frauds, for example. Moreover, the courts will not enforce promises that are against public policy, such as restrictive covenants based upon race, ethnicity or religion.

   b. **Intent To Bind Successors** - The original contracting parties to a real covenant must evince an intention to bind their successors in interest to the land. This is usually done by language in the instrument establishing the covenant. A well-drafted covenant will state the promise is made on behalf of the promisor's "heirs, successors and assigns."

   c. **Touch and Concern Requirement** - To run with the land, a real covenant must affect the value or use of the land or an owner's interest in it. This requirement, that a covenant *touch and concern* the land, prevents a promise that is purely personal and unrelated to the land from being treated as a property right that binds subsequent landowners. A personal promise that does not touch and concern the land is said to be *in gross*.

      The law of real covenants makes distinction between the *benefit* of a promise that runs with the land and the *burden* of a promise that does so. A covenant is said to burden land if it restricts the owner's use of land or reduces its value. Conversely, a covenant benefits land if it enhances its value. As a rule, the party suing on a covenant is seeking to enforce the benefit of the covenant against the defendant who has the burden.

      Some courts will not enforce the burden of a covenant against a subsequent owner of the land if the benefit of the covenant is *in gross*.

Example: A builder, A, sells an unimproved lot to B. The deed to the lot contains a covenant stated to be binding on successors to the land. The covenant requires that any improvements to the lot will be built by A. B later sells the lot to C. C hires another builder to construct her house. A sues C to enforce the benefit of the covenant. A court held on these facts that the burden of the covenant did not run so as to bind C. The court reasoned that the benefit, A's right to build any improvements, was personal to A. It did not benefit any parcel of land and thus did not touch and concern the land. ***Caullett v. Stanley Stilwell & Sons, Inc.***, 67 N.J. Super. 111 (1961).

d. **Privity** - There are two kinds of privity relevant to the law of real covenants. *Horizontal privity* refers to the relationship between the parties who originally agreed to a covenant. *Vertical privity* refers to the relationship between those parties and their successors in interest to the land.

1. **Horizontal Privity** - In order for the burden of a covenant to run with the land, the parties who originally agreed to the covenant must have shared some interest in the land. In the majority of states, there is sufficient horizontal privity between them if the parties have successive interests in the land, i.e., there is a conveyance between them. Under the more restrictive Massachusetts rule, the parties must hold some simultaneous interest in the land.

   Example: A and B are neighbors. They mutually agree that neither will allow a pork rendering plant to be operated on their land. The agreement is in writing, it purports to bind their successors in the land, and is promptly recorded. B sells his land to C who proceeds to operate a pork rendering plant on the site. A may not be able to recover damages from C because there was no horizontal privity between A and B. They did not have a successive or a simultaneous interest in the land.

   Horizontal privity is not generally required for the benefit to run. In other words, a successor to one of the original contracting parties can enforce the burden of the covenant against the remaining original party.

   Example: Assume in the last example, that A started to operate a pork rendering plant on his land after B had sold his property to C. C could obtain money damages from A. This fact pattern involves the benefit running, not the burden, and horizontal privity is not generally required.

2. **Vertical Privity** - A transferee of one of the original contracting parties will be bound by the burden of a covenant only if the transferee succeeds to the entire estate of that party. For the benefit of the covenant to run, the law only requires that the successor succeed to some interest in the land.

   Example: A sells the lot next door to his home to B. B's deed contains a covenant that neither he nor any of his successors will ever permit the property to be used as anything other than a single-family dwelling. B builds a house on the lot and later leases the house to C on a year to year lease. C and her family move in. Later, C's friend, D, and his family move in. A cannot enforce the covenant against multi-family use against C even if the covenant has been breached. There is insufficient vertical privity for the burden of the covenant to run. C did not succeed to B's entire estate. If A, on the other hand, had breached the covenant, C could enforce it against A, because there is sufficient vertical privity for the benefit to run. C need not succeed to B's entire estate for the benefit to run.

e. **Modern Litigation Over Real Covenants** - There is relatively little litigation seeking to enforce covenants at law today. Most persons aggrieved by a breach of covenant seek to enjoin its violation rather than seek money damages. Most reported decisions, therefore, discuss the law of equitable servitudes.

Modern cases involving real covenants, however, have tended to relax the traditional rules. For example, traditionally the courts were reluctant to enforce affirmative obligations as real covenants. As noted above, they also required vertical privity and formulated the rule that the burden of a covenant will not run if the benefit is in gross. Modern decisions have not always hewed to these restrictions.

Example: A real estate developer builds a subdivision with parks and scenic lanes. Covenants in the deeds to every lot in the subdivision require the owner to pay an annual fee to a homeowner's association formed by the developer in order to maintain the parks and lanes. The association does not hold any property in the subdivision. Modern cases have required the fees to be paid by subsequent landowners in the subdivision even though: (1) the payment of money is an affirmative obligation; (2) there is no vertical privity with the homeowner's association because it has not succeeded to any property interest in the subdivision; and (3) the benefit of the fee is arguably in gross in that it is paid to the association. ***Neponsit Property Owners' Association, Inc. v. Emigrant Industrial Savings Bank***, 278 N.Y. 248 (1938).

MBE Advice

Covenants run with the land. Therefore, future owners will be subject to them regardless of whether they were actually aware of them. Watch out for MBE answer choices that try to trick you into letting future owners off the hook because they had no actual knowledge of the covenants. Even if the covenant is not contained in some of the deeds, as long as it is in the public records in the chain of title, subsequent purchasers will be subject to the covenant.

2. **Equitable Servitudes** - When the English courts in equity were asked to enforce covenants, they viewed the privity requirements of the common law as unnecessarily stringent. They ruled that equitable relief to enforce a covenant could be obtained against anyone who had *notice* of the covenant. In the United States, notice is almost available through public title records.

An equitable servitude is thus enforceable if there is (1) an enforceable contract between the original parties to the covenant; (2) which was made by the parties with the intent to bind their successors; (3) with a promise that "touched and concerned" the land; and (4) of which the person to be bound had notice. The elements are identical to those applied by the law courts, except the courts of equity replaced horizontal and vertical privity with the requirement of notice.

Notice can be *actual* or *constructive*. *Record notice*, public filing of a title document that discloses the servitude, will suffice. A servitude will also bind a person with *inquiry* notice of it. A person who wants to put property to a commercial use, for example, has a duty to inquire if the property sits in the middle of a residential neighborhood.

3. **Implied Reciprocal Servitudes** - Courts will indeed imply reciprocal servitudes if a person has *notice* of a *common development plan or scheme* for a neighborhood. The typical case involves a real estate developer who sells some lots in a neighborhood subject to restrictions but who does not restrict the lots not sold. Later purchasers of those lots may be bound even though their deeds are unrestricted.

   Example: A developer purchases a large tract of land. He records a map which divides the tract into half-acre lots. He then advertises "prime building lots in an attractive residential community." He sells a number of lots with deed restrictions that limit use of the lots to single family residences. A buys such a lot. The developer does not restrict the lots he retains. Later, he sells one of those unrestricted lots to B. B's deed has no restriction on use and B begins to build a gas station on the lot. A purchaser of one of the restricted lots in the subdivision, like A, may be able to enjoin B from constructing the gas station. There is evidence of a common development scheme from the map, advertisements, and the nature of the neighborhood. B had record notice of the map and inquiry notice of the residential nature of the subdivision. As such, he could be bound by an implied servitude. ***Sanborn v. McClean***, 233 Mich. 227 (1925).

4. **Termination of Real Covenants and Equitable Servitudes** - Real covenants and equitable servitudes can come to an end for any of the reasons discussed above with regard to easements. A covenant may terminate of its own terms. A person might acquire the benefited and the burdened land and thus extinguish the covenant or servitude by merger. Restrictions can be released or abandoned and so on.

   a. **Changed Circumstances** - Restrictive covenants are often challenged when a neighborhood has markedly changed since the covenants were put in place. Courts will continue to enforce covenants and servitudes, however, even in the face of dramatic change. If the restrictions put in place for a neighborhood still serve their purpose for some residents, the courts will continue to enforce them.

      Example: Fifty years ago, a builder developed a residential subdivision. Restrictions in the deed to each lot in the subdivision limited use of the lot to single family residences. The area surrounding the subdivision has become a major commercial development. The roads bordering the subdivisions which were once two lane roads are now major four lane thoroughfares. It is likely a court would rule the owners of lots in the center of the subdivision still benefit from the restrictions. A court probably would continue to enforce the restrictions because they keep commercial development at some distance from those lots.

b. **Equitable Defenses** - Because persons frequently seek equitable relief for violations of restrictive covenants, the traditional equitable defenses may prevent enforcement of a servitude.

   1) **Laches** - If a person entitled to enforce a servitude delays in seeking relief, a court of equity may deny it.

      Example: The deeds in a subdivision required houses to be set back forty feet from the street. A person delays in seeking to enforce the set back until a house is completely built. A court may deny enforcement.

   2) **Unclean Hands** - A person who is violating deed restrictions cannot expect a court to enforce those same restrictions against others.

   3) **Estoppel** - A person may be estopped from enforcing a covenant if by word or deed that person leads another to rely on the belief that covenant will not be enforced.

   4) **Acquiescence** - If a person knows of and has not objected to violations of a restrictive covenant by others, they cannot suddenly enforce against someone.

      Example: The deeds in a subdivision establish minimum lot sizes for homes. A number of persons in the subdivision, however, have built homes on smaller lots. A homeowner in the subdivision cannot suddenly enforce the restriction against a new buyer.

VII. RIGHTS AND DUTIES INCIDENT TO THE OWNERSHIP OF LAND

According to a central principle of the common law, an owner of the land had the exclusive right to possess everything beneath the surface to the center of the earth, and everything above the surface, to the reaches of the heavens. The principle has been modified since the advent of the air travel. Federal statutes now mandate that the air space above the minimum altitude for flight belongs to the public. Apart from this modification, the common law principle remains largely intact. An owner of land enjoys a number of ancillary property rights. These include rights of support to protect the land from subsidence, rights in water, and rights in personal property affixed to the land.

A. RIGHT TO SUPPORT

The law protects owners and possessors of land from the danger of subsidence by a neighbor on the surface or the owner of a subsurface estate. The support each piece of land gives neighboring parcels is called *lateral support*. The support underground layers give the surface is called *subjacent support*.

1. **Lateral Support** - An owner or possessor of land had the right to have their land supported in its natural state by neighboring parcels. The law protects the right with a strict liability rule. A person who deprives a landowner of lateral support is liable for the ensuing damage without regard to negligence. The major limitation on the right of lateral support is that it extends only to land in its natural condition unburdened by buildings or other improvements. If land is improved, the plaintiff in a lateral support action must prove the land would have subsided if it were not improved, or must prove the defendant was negligent.

2. **Subjacent Support** - The owner or possessor of the surface of land is also entitled to have the land supported from below. If the occupant of the underlying strata undermines the surface, the occupant will be strictly liable for the damage caused. Although there is authority to the contrary, the duty of subjacent support extends only to owner and occupiers of the substrata. An action for subjacent support will not lie, for example, if subsidence is caused by pumping water from an underground aquifer. The law of subjacent support is identical to the law of lateral support with one exception. Some courts hold a subsurface owner is liable for subsidence of improved land if the improvements were on the land before severance of the subsurface estate.

   Example: A owns a farm, Blackacre, improved with a house, barn and silo. A leases the subsurface of Blackacre to a mining company. The mining company began mining under Blackacre. Through no fault of the mining company, the surface of Blackacres subsides. The mining company may be strictly liable for the subsidence even though Blackacre was improved. The structures were on the land before the severance of the mining rights from rights to the surface.

3. **Negligence** - Even though an action for support may not lie, a person who causes subsidence may be liable under ordinary tort principles for negligence.

   Example: There are three contiguous lots running from east to west on Maple Street. While undertaking an excavation, the owner of the easternmost lot, A, causes the other two lots to subside. The owner of the westernmost lot, C, had built a house on his lot and the subsidence damaged the foundation of the building. C probably does not have an action for support against A for two reasons. First, only the owners of neighboring parcels have the duty to give lateral support. Second, C's lot was improved and it might be difficult to show the subsidence would have occurred had there been no house on the lot. C may have an action against A, however, if A was negligent in not shoring the excavation.

B. WATER RIGHTS

The common law established different rules for water that flowed in a natural watercourse; water that percolated from underneath the surface; and run-off, surface water not confined to a stream or other body of water.

1. **Riparian Rights** - The law of *riparian rights* governs water that runs in a river, stream, or other natural watercourse. Only property owners with land on the stream enjoy riparian rights. At common law, every riparian owner could draw water off from the stream for domestic use without liability to downstream owners. Any other use, however, could not diminish the *natural flow* of the stream as to its quality, volume or velocity. The natural flow theory did not allow much industrial development. As a result, all states, adopted a reasonableness test. Under this test, a riparian owner is liable to others downstream only if the owner unreasonably diminishes the quality, volume or velocity of the water.

   The same rules apply to water in natural lakes and ponds. The rights to lake and pond water are more properly called *littoral rights.*

2. **Underground or Percolating Water -** Water beneath the surface of the earth in underground aquifers can reach the surface through a natural spring or an artificial well. In either case, the common law applied a rule of capture. The owner of the surface was entitled to draw off as much underground water as he or she wished. There was no liability to other landowners whose property lay over the same water table. The only limitation on a surface owner's right to draw off underground water was that the owner's neighbors had the same right. Most American jurisdictions have rejected the English Rule with regard to underground water in favor of a rule of correlative rights. **Under the modern American approach, surface owners are entitled to a reasonable use of the underground water.** They can be liable for unreasonably diminishing their neighbors' access to a common pool.

   Example: The owner of a limestone quarry pumps water from an underground aquifer to use in the quarrying operations. As a result, other landowners' wells run dry. The quarry owner may be liable to the other landowners under a rule of correlative rights. ***Cline v. American Aggregates Corporation***, 15 Ohio St.3d 384 (1984).

3. **Diffuse Surface Water** - The English courts applied the *common enemy doctrine* to rainwater or snow melt running off the surface of the land. A landowner was privileged to divert run-off, even onto a neighbor's land. Liability would arise only if the owner diverted with the purpose of injuring. In this respect, the common enemy doctrine resembled the law of *spite fences*. There was generally no liability for building a fence even if it shaded a neighbor's garden unless the fence was built with malice or spite.

   Example: In an effort to avoid dampness in her basement, A builds a retaining wall in her garden. The wall causes rainwater to run-off onto B's lawn making it very soggy most of the Spring. A would not be liable to B under the common enemy doctrine because she did not build the wall to injure B.

C. FIXTURES

Personal property or chattels can be attached to real estate. As a result, an owner of the real estate often has a claim to the personal property under the law of *fixtures.*

1. **"Fixture" Defined** - A fixture is personal property that has become affixed to real property in such as to be deemed a part of the real property. The majority of American jurisdictions look at three factors to determine whether or not goods have become fixtures:

   a. **Annexation** - The courts will examine the extent to which the personal property has been firmly affixed to the real estate. The more difficult an item is to remove, the more likely it is to be a fixture. Most courts, for example, would find a furnace sunk in concrete to be a fixture.

   b. **Adaptation to the Use of the Real Property** - The courts will also examine how well adapted the personal property has become to the use of the real estate. A water heater once it is connected to the water and gas lines of a home becomes central to the use of the home as a residence. It is treated as a fixture at that point.

   c. **Intent of the Parties** - The intention of the parties who affix the goods to the real property may be relevant. Intentions expressed in an agreement, however, cannot frustrate the expectations of a third party who was not privy to the contract:

   Example: The owner of a motor hotel purchases a number of heating and air conditioning units of the type that fit into a hole in the wall of each hotel room. The owner agrees to pay for the units in installments. The sales agreement specifies that the units are not intended to become fixtures. The intention expressed in the agreement has no bearing on the rights of the mortgagee of the hotel building. The mortgagee was not a party to the contract and would expect the units to be fixtures. They were firmly attached to the building. Their removal would leave the building full of holes. Moreover, the were central to the use of the real estate. ***Lewiston Bottled Gas Company v. Key Bank***, 601 A.2d 91 (Maine 1992).

   In other words, in looking for intention, the courts ask: would the ordinary, reasonable person assume the article in question is part of the real estate?

2. **Rights of the Owner of the Realty** - Once an item has become a fixture, it becomes part of the real estate. The item cannot be removed without liability to the owner of the real property or a person holding a mortgage on the real property. There are some exceptions to this rule:

   a. **Landlord and Tenant** - The law permits commercial tenants to remove *trade fixtures* without liability to the landlord. Trade fixture are chattels used to carry out the tenant's trade or business. The American courts have permitted tenants to do the same with agricultural fixtures, sheds, chicken coops and the like. Modern decisions permit tenants to remove replacements of domestic appliances and ornaments purchased by residential tenants during their term.

Example: A mechanic, A, leases space for a machine shop from a landlord, B. A installs a lathe in the shop. The lathe is quite heavy. It is bolted to floor and directly connected to the electrical wiring of the shop. The lathe is a trade fixture and thus can be removed by A even though it is firmly affixed to the real property.

b. **Licensees and Trespassers** - Licensees are sometimes given permission to erect small structures or attach items of personal property to the land. Such permission by the landowner gives rise to implied consent to the structure or fixture once the license has expired. Trespassers, on the other hand, generally lose the right to remove personal property they have attached to another's land without permission.
Example: A owns land next to the county fair grounds. In return for an agreed fee, A lets B erect a refreshment stand on his property during the days of the fair. As a licensee, B can remove the stand at the close of the fair. The result would be different if B erected the stand without A's permission. B would then be a trespasser.

c. **Secured Transactions** - A person with a security interest in personal property under Article Nine of the Uniform Commercial Code may enjoy priority over the owner or mortgagee of the real estate by making a fixture filing under Article Nine. *See,* UCC §9-334(d).

d. **Removal** - A tenant or a secured party that has a right to remove a fixture can be liable to the owner of the real property for damage done to the real estate during removal. Under the Uniform Commercial Code, the owner of the real estate may require a bond or other security for the costs to repair any physical injury done to the real property upon removal. UCC §9-604(d).

VIII. ADVERSE POSSESSION

A person may acquire title to real property by long, uninterrupted possession adverse to the interest of the owner. Title by adverse possession results from the expiration of the statute of limitations applicable to the owner's action to recover the property. A seventeenth century statute set the common law limitations period at 20 years.

A. ELEMENTS OF ADVERSE POSSESSION

Over the years, judicial decisions have developed rules and principles that supplement the statute.

1. **Actual Entry** - Judicial decisions have made clear the statute does not begin to run until there has been an *actual entry* against the owner. If an adverse possessor enters and occupies only part of a larger parcel of land, the possessor will generally acquire title only to that part.

2. **Adversity or Hostility** - The person in possession of the property must be acting adversely to the interest of the owner. A person who enters with the owner's permission, a tenant or licensee, does not enter adversely to the interest of the owner. The requirement that the possession be *adverse* or *hostile* also generally prevents a concurrent owner from acquiring exclusive title by adverse possession even if the owner is in sole possession of the property. Each concurrent owner is entitled to possession of the whole. Unless one co-tenant has ousted another, the co-tenant's possession is not adverse to other.

3. **Claim of Right** - The courts have often stated that an adverse possessor acts under *claim of right.* In most states, this requirement means simply that the person intends to appropriate and use the land as that person's own. In other words, the possessor acts like the owner. The phrase "claim of right" does not refer to the possessor's motives. A person may acquire title to land by adverse possession even if the person knows they are occupying the land of another. In the majority of states, good faith is not required.

4. **Exclusivity** - Because the owner of land must have the ability to bring a lawsuit against an identifiable person, adverse possession cannot vest title in the public. For this reason, the courts have ruled that adverse possession must be *exclusive*, not shared with the public generally. The requirement that possession be exclusive does not bar two, three or even more people from acquiring title by adverse possession as co-tenants. The owner after all could name multiple defendants in an ejectment action.

   The courts have also ruled that possession cannot be shared with the owner probably for the reason that shared possession is unlikely to be hostile.

5. **Open and Notorious** - The courts have required that adverse possession be open and notorious. This element requires acts of possession that put the owner on notice so the owner can bring the ejectment action.

   Example: The owner of Blackacre, A, is unaware that B has opened a lateral mineshaft under Blackacre. B works the mine continuously for twenty-two years. A probably can nevertheless still eject B. B's possession of the substrata was not open and notorious.

6. **Continuity** - The courts have generally required that a person be in continuous possession of property throughout the limitations period in order to acquire title by adverse possession. If possession is interrupted for any length of time, the statute begins to run anew when the possessor returns. The requirement prevents intermittent use from rising to adverse possession. It does not require the possessor occupy the land every minute of every day. For example, courts have awarded title to vacation property to a person who occupied the property every season. The test is whether the occupancy was of a character suited to the property.

B. TACKING

The courts have permitted an adverse possessor to tack his or her period of possession with that of an earlier possessor. The courts do require privity between the adverse possessor and his or her predecessor, in order to tack their periods of possession.

Example: A is the owner of Blackacre in fee simple when B enters into possession of the property. B occupies Blackacre for fifteen years when he sells whatever interest he has in Blackacre to C. C enters into possession and remains on Blackacre for six years. C is the owner of Blackacre by adverse possession. His six years of possession can be tacked with B's fifteen years. B and C were in privity. The common law, twenty year period of limitations has run on A's right to recover possession.

C. COLOR OF TITLE

A person takes possession of land under color of title if they act under a deed or other instrument which purports to confer title but which is in fact legally ineffective. Color of title is not generally required for effective adverse possession. It can, however, give the person claiming under a faulty instrument constructive possession of all the land the instrument purports to convey.

Example: A purchases Blackacre from B, a person who claims to be acting for the record owner of Blackacre, C. A receives a deed from B bearing a forgery of C's signature. A enters into possession of a portion of Blackacre and remains there for twenty years. During that time, A never cultivates or improves most of the acreage described in her deed. Under the rules outlined above, A would normally be able to claim title to only that land she actually possessed. She has, however, color of title through the forged deed and may be awarded all the land described in the deed.

D. TOLLING

In many states, the limitations period in ejectment does not run against an owner of property who is under a legal disability when an adverse possessor enters into possession. By statute, the limitations period is tolled until the owner's disability is removed. Generally, the limitations period is tolled, however, only if the owner is under a disability at the time of entry which is deemed when the cause of action for ejectment accrues.
Example: A owns Blackacre. B enters into possession adversely to A's interest in 1980. Two years later, A suffers a severe mental illness and is adjudicated as incompetent. If B remains in possession, he will have title to Blackacre in 2000. The statute is not tolled for A who was of sound mind when B entered.

The courts do not tack disabilities.

Example: A, who is of unsound mind, owns Blackacre in fee simple absolute. B enters into possession adversely to A's interest in 1980. A dies, still legally incompetent, in 1995. A's sole heir at law is a child, C, who is ten years old in 1995. In most jurisdictions, the statute of limitation will begin running against C even though she is a minor. The limitations period will be tolled for A's disability which existed when the cause of action accrued, not C's, which did not arise until later.

IX. CONVEYANCES OF LAND

The typical land sale involves several stages. First, the buyer (or vendee) and the seller (or vendor) reach an agreement on the essential terms of the sale. This agreement is put in writing as the statute of frauds requires in a document called a *contract for sale of land.* The contract sets a time and place for *closing*, usually within the next few months. At closing, the buyer must pay for the property and, in return, the seller must tender a *deed* to the buyer. In the interim, the buyer must obtain financing which is generally done by giving a lender a *mortgage* on the property. Both the buyer and the mortgage lender, have an interest in making sure the seller's title to the property is sound. Every sale of land involves an investigation of the quality of the seller's title based primarily upon instruments publicly recorded with the Recorder of Deeds.

A. CONTRACTS FOR SALE

A land sale agreement must be an enforceable contract. For example, a person who offers to sell his home in an evident joke is not contractually bound when someone snaps up the offer. A land sale contract must be supported by consideration. It must be definite enough to enable the court to fashion a remedy. It can be avoided for fraud, duress, or lack of legal capacity. Extrinsic evidence that varies or contradicts the contract may be barred under the parol evidence rule and so on. Some issues involving land sale contracts, however, are unique.

1. **Statute of Frauds** - A contract for sale of land must be in a signed writing that sets forth the essential terms of the parties' agreement. Grants of easements, real covenants, mortgage agreements, and leases longer than a year must also be in writing. There are two major exceptions to the statute of frauds.

   a. **Part Performance** - The courts may enforce an oral agreement if one of the parties has rendered a performance that is unequivocally related to the making of the agreement. In a sale of land, payment of the purchase price standing alone is not enough to make a oral land contract enforceable (although the aggrieved party may have an action for restitution). The courts generally require additional evidence of performance, such as the entry into possession or the making of improvements.

   b. **Estoppel** - A party may be estopped to repudiate an oral agreement upon which the other party has substantially and detrimentally relied. As noted above, an oral grant of easement may be enforced if the grantee has relied on the grant to his or her detriment.

2. **Equitable Conversion** - The law considers land to be unique. In the eyes of the law, a person aggrieved by a breach of a contract of sale cannot be made whole by an award of money damages. Therefore, the court's action in equity will enforce a contract of sale through a decree of specific performance. Because the buyer of land can obtain such a decree, the equitable title to the land is deemed to have passed to the buyer once the parties have entered a contract for sale. The seller's interest, the right to the agreed purchase price, is considered personal property. Bare legal title remains with the seller until closing but the seller is deemed to hold this title in trust for the buyer as security for the agreed price.

a. **Death** - The doctrine of equitable conversion has ramifications when one of the parties dies after a land sale contract is signed but before closing.

Example: A enters into a contract to sell Blackacre to B. A dies before closing, leaving a will. The will devises all A's real property to C and bequeaths all A's personal property to D. Under the doctrine of equitable conversion, A had no real property which would pass to C under the Will. D will receive the sales proceeds. If B had died, B's heirs or devisees could specifically enforce the contract to receive title at the agreed closing date. In the eyes of the law, B had equitable title to the real property which would pass to his heirs or devisees.

b. **Casualty Loss** - The courts also look to the doctrine of equitable conversion in allocating the risk of a casualty loss between the parties when they have not provided for the risk in the contract. Because title is deemed to have passed to the buyer upon execution of the contract, the majority of jurisdictions hold the buyer bears the risk of loss due to fire, floods and other casualty losses. If the seller collects insurance due to the loss, he or she must credit the buyer with the insurance proceeds because the seller holds legal title in trust for the buyer.

3. **Closing Date** - The contract of sale generally establishes a closing date but the courts do not consider the date to be material unless the agreement clearly states "time is of the essence."

4. **Marketable Title** - Implied in every contract for sale of land is an obligation on the part of the seller to deliver marketable title to the buyer. Marketable title does not mean perfect title but rather, title reasonably free from doubt or the threat of litigation. The following defects in title would render title unmarketable:

a. ***Servitudes*** - Any easement, profit, real covenant or other servitude would constitute an encumbrance that would render title unmarketable;

b. ***Liens*** - Any unsatisfied mortgage, mechanic's lien, tax lien or other charge on the land would justify the buyer in rejecting title;

c. ***Title Problems*** - Any defect in the chain of title, such as a defectively executed or unrecorded deed, will render title unmarketable. Title acquired by adverse possession is considered unmarketable in the majority of states until a quiet title action settles record title in the possessor;

d. ***Land Description*** - A discrepancy in the record as to the land conveyed will breach the obligation.

e. ***Violation of Statutes, Regulations and Ordinances*** - Restrictions in statutes and ordinances are *not* deemed encumbrances that render unmarketable but an *existing violation* of a zoning ordinance is usually held to breach the warranty;

Example: A agrees to sell a house and lot to B. The property is subject to zoning regulations that limit its use to residential purposes and require a minimum lot size for building a house. B discovers the lot was smaller than the minimum. B can refuse to close on the basis of the violation of the minimum lot size. That portion of the zoning ordinance was violated. The restriction on use is not an encumbrance.
If title is unmarketable, the buyer must give the seller a reasonable time to cure the defect. Remember, unless otherwise stated in the contract time is not of the essence. Moreover, the seller is entitled to satisfy a mortgage or other lien on the land with the proceeds of the sale. If the proceeds will satisfy the mortgage or lien and clear the title at closing, the buyer cannot claim title is unmarketable.

MBE Advice

You may encounter a scenario on the MBE in which the seller has actually breached the contract by not clearing all encumbrances prior to the closing. Keep in mind that in spite of the fact that the buyer may be in breach of contract, he/she still has the right to complete the sale and use the proceeds to clear the title.

Similarly, you may encounter a situation where the grantor claims to have good title but does not actually have it at the time of transfer. A related doctrine provides that if the grantor acquires good title at a later time, the property is automatically transferred to the grantee, and the grantor is estopped from later denying the effectiveness of his/her deed.

The implied warranty that title is marketable can be modified in the agreement of sale. It is customary, for example, to except recorded easements and the like, from the warranty. The parties might also agree to a different standard such as "insurable" title or indeed, may disclaim any obligation on the seller's part for title quality at all. Remember, however, that the implied obligation to deliver marketable title arises unless clearly stated otherwise. It arises even if the seller promises the buyer only a quitclaim deed at closing.

Courts have ruled that a buyer impliedly agreed to accept visible easements from the seller's warranty of marketable title. This is particularly true of public roads or streets.

5. **Remedies** - A breach of a contract for sale of land gives rise to unique remedies. As noted above, a buyer is entitled to a decree in specific performance against the seller who refuses to deliver title at closing. By the same token, the seller can bring an action for the price against the recalcitrant buyer. Thus, unlike most contracts, courts will enforce a land sale contract by ordering the parties to perform.

   If this is impossible, as it is when the seller cannot deliver marketable title, the courts will award damages. As a general rule, the standard "loss of bargain" measure of contract damages applies. A buyer should receive the difference between the agreed contract price and the market value of the land on the date of closing. About half the states, however, apply a restitutionary measure of recovery if the seller in good faith cannot deliver marketable title.

Example: A contracted to sell Blackacre to B. B paid $1,000 down and agreed to pay the balance at closing. One of A's predecessors in title had acquired Blackacre at a sheriff's sale. A person with an interest in the property was never notified of the sale or the legal proceedings giving rise to it. As a result, that person has the sale set aside shortly after A and B enter the contract of sale. As a result, A cannot deliver marketable title to B. B may be limited to recovery of her $1,000 payment. A acted in good faith. A did not know of the defect. He did not cause it and could not cure it.

Sales contracts for land typically require the buyer to make a down payment on the purchase price, usually called *earnest money.* Contracts frequently provide the seller may retain the earnest money as liquidated damages in the event the buyer fails to close. Courts enforce such clauses unless the amount involved unreasonably exceeds the seller's anticipated damages.

6. **Defects in the Condition of the Property** - At common law, under the rule of *caveat emptor*, a seller of real property was not liable to the buyer for the physical condition of the property absent affirmative fraud. In recent years, the law of *caveat emptor* has undergone change both in the courts and the state legislatures.

   a. **New Construction** - Most jurisdictions today recognize an implied warranty of fitness and quality in the sale of a newly constructed home. Many of the jurisdictions that recognize the warranty, however, permit only the builder's immediate buyer to sue on the warranty.

   b. **Mandatory Disclosure Statutes** - Many jurisdictions have enacted statutes that require certain mandatory disclosures. These statutes often require a seller of real property to complete and give the buyer a form that discloses all material matters related to the physical condition of the property that are known to the seller. These form typically treat as material the source of the water supply to the home, the means of sewage disposal, the presence of any hazardous substance, such as asbestos or radon, and the condition of the roof, floors, walls and foundation.

   c. **Developments in Judicial Decisions** - The courts have increasingly found liability for non-disclosure of material defects. Most jurisdictions now recognize a seller can be liable for a negligent misrepresentation of a material fact relied upon by the buyer. Some courts today also recognize an affirmative duty on the part of the seller to disclose any material defect the seller is aware of that would not be revealed upon an inspection of the property. Finally, the seller is liable for deceit which may include acts of concealing a known defect in addition to affirmative misrepresentations.

B. THE DEED

At closing, the seller tenders a deed to the buyer which triggers the buyer's obligation to pay the agreed purchase price. The law has established formal requirements for a deed to take effect. Deeds also set forth warranties as to title quality.

1. **Formal Requirements** - A deed transfers title to land and must be in writing under the statute of frauds. The grantor must sign the deed, and the deed must identify the parties and describe the land.

   a. **Forgeries** - A forged deed is void. If the grantor's signature is forged, the deed is wholly ineffective to pass the grantor's interest. If the deed is procured by fraud, the courts generally make a distinction between *real fraud* and *fraud in the inducement.* Real fraud involves deception that prevents the grantor from knowing what the grantor is signing. Fraud in the inducement is deceit that leads the grantor to sign the deed but which does not mislead the grantor as to the nature of the document.

   Real fraud, sometimes called *fraud in the factum,* is rare but, where it is found, it voids a deed. Fraud in the inducement, however, makes the deed voidable. The distinction is important if the wrongdoer sells the property to a good faith purchaser. A good faith purchaser can acquire good title from a wrongdoer who acquired it through fraud in the inducement and held voidable title. A good faith purchaser cannot acquire title from a wrongdoer who obtained a deed through real fraud.

   Example: A owns Blackacre. One afternoon when A is in a hurry, B asks A to sign a innocuous petition. Unbeknownst to A, B conceals carbon paper and a form deed to Blackacre under the petition. B immediately records the deed and sells Blackacre to C who pays a fair price for the property without any notice of how B obtained his deed. A can claim Blackacre from C even though C is a good faith purchaser for value. A signed the deed as a result of real fraud. He did not know what he was signing nor did he have a reasonable opportunity to know what he was signing.

   b. **The Property Description** - An exact description of the property conveyed is not required in a deed. The description must be definite enough to allow a court to fashion a remedy in the case of a dispute. There must be enough of a description to enable the court to identify the tract conveyed from all the other parcels of land in the world. The description may require extrinsic evidence. For example, a description by reference to a map has been held sufficient even though the map is not recorded. The courts have also enforced omnibus or "Mother Hubbard" clauses, i.e., "all my land in Franklin County." Because deeds requiring extrinsic evidence create havoc for title examiners, however, some jurisdictions treat such deeds as unrecorded under the recording acts. In these jurisdictions, such a deed is effective between the immediate parties but not a subsequent good faith purchaser.

The three methods most commonly used to describe land are by reference to: (1) **the United States Government Survey System;** (2) **a recorded map called a *plat*;** and (3) a **metes and bounds survey**. The methods are not mutually exclusive. A person may use a plat, for example, to locate a point for beginning a metes and bounds description.

Example: Consider the following metes and bounds description of the six-sided tract of land illustrated below:

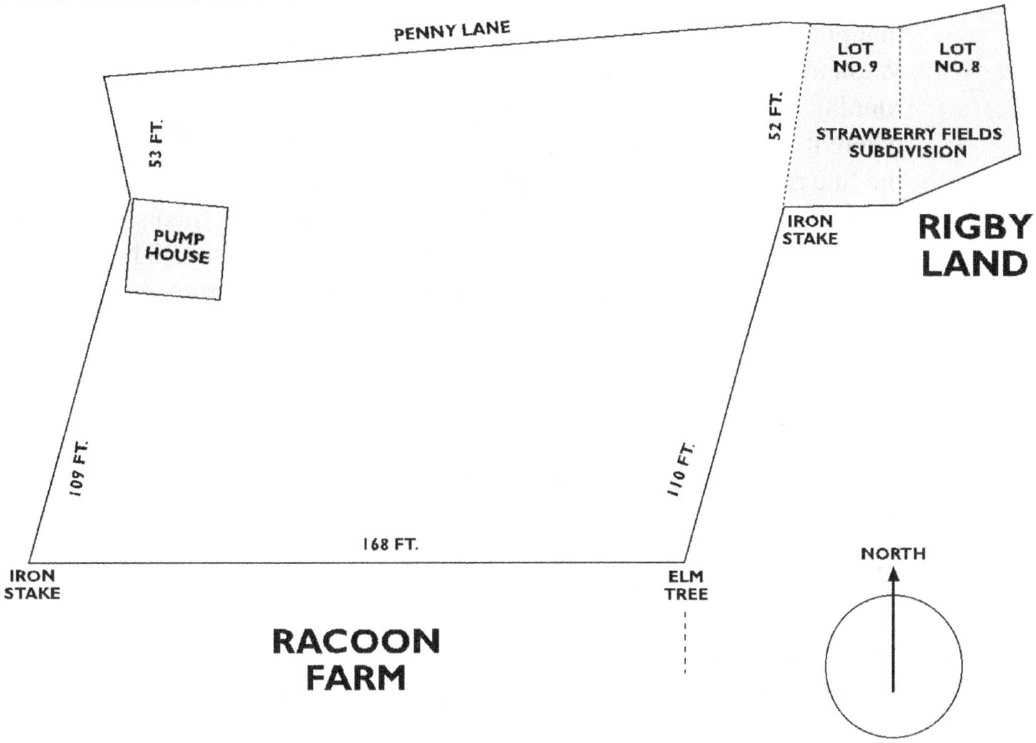

Beginning at the point of the northwest corner of Lot No. 9, Block A, in the Strawberry Fields Subdivision as shown in Plat Book C, page 16, Recorder of Deeds, Liverpool, Ohio, continuing South 15° 50' 10" West along the line of said lot and the property now or formerly of Eleanor Rigby a distance of 52 feet to an iron stake; thence South 20° 00' 00" West a distance of 110 feet to a large elm tree; thence North 89°, 21' 00" West along the line of the property now or formerly of Rocco Racoon a distance of 168 feet to an iron stake; thence North 20° 00' 00" East a distance of 109 feet to the northwest corner of a pump house; thence North 15° 50' 10" West a distance of 53 feet to a point on the south side of Penny Lane; thence along the south side of said lane to the point or place of beginning.

A metes and bounds description outlines the perimeter of a tract by measures of distance (the "metes") and boundaries (the "bounds") that begin at a single point and run along compass headings (called "courses") until the line described returns to the beginning. In the example, the starting point is provided by reference to a recorded map or plat of a subdivision. The first course taken from that point runs South 15 degrees, 50 minutes, 10 seconds West. This means that the boundary in this area runs south southwest from the starting point. Imagine a line running true south from the starting point, the northwest corner of Lot Number 9. The boundary on this part of the tract lies west of that imaginary line by 50 degrees, 50 minutes, 10 seconds. (A minute is 1/60th of a degree and a second is 1/60th of a minute.) The first course runs for a distance of 52 feet to an iron stake driven into the ground when the land was surveyed. At that point, the boundary line shifts and begins to run 20 degrees west of true south, a little more than four degrees further west than the first course. The boundary here runs a distance of 110 feet to an elm tree marked by the surveyor. At that point, the boundary runs westward. The course described, North 89°, 21' 00" West, means the boundary runs nearly ninety degrees west of an imaginary line running due north from the elm tree. The boundary runs in this direction for 168 feet where it reaches another iron stake the surveyor drove into the ground. At that point, the line runs twenty degrees east of true north for a distance of 109 feet until it meets the northwest corner of the pump house. The boundary then shifts somewhat to the west for a distance of 53 feet where it reaches Penny Lane. The southern side of Penny Lane marks the remaining boundary line, which runs east to the beginning point.

When the boundary of a parcel of land is described by reference to a stream, the meandering of the stream over time may change the physical boundary. As the stream slowly deposits silt on one bank, it will enlarge the land owned by the property owner with to that bank. The slow deposit of soil in this fashion is called *accretion* and it will result in a shifting of the boundary line. *Avulsion*, a sudden change in the course of the stream, will not shift the boundary.

c. **The Identification of the Parties** - In the majority of jurisdictions a deed must identify the grantee in order to pass title. Extrinsic evidence, however, can be admitted to identify the grantee.

Example: A prepares a deed granting Blackacre to "my daughter" without any further reference to her identity. Extrinsic evidence could be admitted to show A had one daughter, B.

In most jurisdictions, the grantee can complete a form deed in which the space for the grantee's name was inadvertently left blank.

2. **Delivery** - A deed passes title upon its *delivery* and acceptance. To make a legally effective delivery, the grantor must intend to make a present transfer of an interest in the property. Delivery is presumed if: (1) the grantee has possession of the deed; (2) the grantor acknowledges delivery before a notary public; or (3) the deed is duly recorded. There is a presumption of non-delivery if the grantor never relinquishes possession of the deed. All these presumptions may be rebutted.

MBE Advice

The law governing the transfer of deeds is frequently tested on the MBE. In order for title to property to be validly conveyed, the deed must be delivered. The question of whether delivery has occurred will depend primarily upon the intent of the grantor. The deed will not be considered "delivered" until such time that the grantor actually intends to convey an immediate and irrevocable interest to the grantee.

Examples: A prepared a deed granting title to his summer cottage to his daughter, B. A gave B the keys to the cottage and had the utilities transferred to her name. A also had his daughter's name put on the mailbox and notified the post office that he would no longer be residing at the cottage. A, however, inadvertently forgot to deliver or record the deed. Later, A died. The deed was found among his papers. Although A's retention of the deed would raise a presumption of non-delivery, the presumption could be rebutted by evidence of B's other acts which demonstrated a present intention to transfer title.

The presumption arising from the grantee's possession of the deed could also be rebutted. Assume A prepared the deed in the Spring but did not intend to transfer title to the cottage to B until the end of the Summer. In the early Spring, A gave B a number of his papers which as a result of an oversight included the deed A had prepared. A could testify, in a suit to quiet title brought by B, that he did not intend to transfer title to B when he gave her the deed.

If the grantor of a deed retains an unconditional power to revoke or recall it, some courts will hold the deed does not evince a present intention to transfer title and will not enforce it even if the grantor has handed over to the grantee. The retained power to revoke or recall the deed negates delivery.

3. **Acceptance** - A deed must be accepted by the grantee. In most states, acceptance is presumed if the property is of value to the grantee. The chief purpose of this requirement is to allow the grantee to refuse an unwanted conveyance. Once a deed is accepted by the grantee, however, he or she cannot convey it back to the grantor by handing it back, nor can he or she negate its legal effect by destroying it.

Watch Out!

Destruction of a deed does **not** cause title to revert to the original owner. A deed is only evidence of title. Once a deed has been delivered and accepted, the original owner has no further claim to it.

Example: A prepares a deed to his summer cottage which he gives to his daughter, B. Sometime later, A asks B to give the cottage back and B dutifully gives her father back the deed. B still has title to the cottage. B acquired title upon delivery and acceptance of the deed. To reconvey title, B must prepare her own deed to A. Remember all transfers of interests in land must comply with the statute of frauds and other formalities required of conveyances.

4. **Conditional Delivery and Use of A Deed As A Will Substitute** - The law generally will not enforce oral conditions given upon delivery of a deed that is unconditional on its face. **Example:** A prepares an unconditional deed to his summer cottage naming his daughter, B, as grantee. When A gives the deed to B, he says, "the cottage is yours once you pass the bar examination." Most courts would not admit evidence of this statement as a oral condition that contradicts the deed. For the same reason, the evidence would also be inadmissible to rebut the presumption of delivery arising from B's possession of the deed. In the majority of jurisdictions, B would have title to the cottage whether or not she passes the bar exam. Note if the condition had been written into the deed, A would have conveyed an executory interest to B. This would be a perfectly valid present transfer of a future interest by deed.

   If a deed states it will not take effect until the death of the grantor, the courts may not enforce it. Such a deed arguably does not make a present transfer of an interest in property and therefore is not legally "delivered". Such a deed may also run afoul of the statute of wills which requires a document which conforms with its provisions to make a testamentary disposition. A deed like this, however, is distinguishable from one that makes a present transfer of a future interest.

   Example: A prepares a deed to his summer cottage, which he gives to his daughter, B. In the deed, A retains a life estate, with a remainder to B. A has made a perfectly valid *inter vivos* transfer of a remainder to B and the deed would be enforceable. If A, on the other hand, had prepared a deed which stated it would "take effect on my death," a court could view that language as testamentary and void. It could also hold the language negates delivery. This approach strikes some courts and many commentators as overly formalistic and one that works a trap for the unsophisticated. They would read both deeds to convey a remainder to B.

5. **Delivery to a Third Party** - A grantor can deliver a deed through a third person. Evidence, however, that the grantor retained the power to recall the deed from the third person will negate delivery. Such a power may be inferred from the fact that the third person was the agent of the grantor.

   If the grantor delivers a deed to a third party with conditional instructions to deliver it at a later time to the grantee, the courts will usually enforce those conditions even if they are not in writing.

Example: A prepares an unconditional deed to his summer cottage naming his daughter, B, as grantee. A gives the deed to C and tells C to give the deed to B "once she passes the bar examination." Most courts would admit evidence of this statement. The deed has not yet been delivered to B, so there is no presumption arising from delivery. C or anyone else can testify as to the instructions given C.

Instructions given to a third party to deliver a deed to the grantee in the event of the grantor's death, however, may run afoul of the statute of wills and may negate delivery if the grantor retains the power to recall the deed from the third party. Traditionally, the courts will enforce such instructions only if the grantor has irrevocably transferred the deed to the third party.

6. **Escrow Agents** - In sales, as opposed to gifts of real estate, a disinterested third party, called an *escrow agent*, is often used to facilitate the satisfactory performance of conditions to a sale.

   Example: A agrees to exchange Blackacre for 1,000 shares of XYZ Corporation stock. To facilitate the exchange, A may prepare and deliver a deed to an escrow agent with instructions to deliver it to XYZ Corporation upon transfer of the shares to A's broker.

   When the conditions to an escrow have been met and the deed has been delivered to the grantee, the grantee's title is generally considered to have passed at the time the escrow agent took possession of the deed. This *relation back* feature of an escrow can be useful. If the grantor dies, for example, after delivery of the deed to the escrow agent, the closing can occur without the need to find heirs or devisees and have them execute the deed.

   There are two requirement for true escrows: (1) there must be a written contract of sale or written instructions stating the conditions for delivery of the deed to the grantee; (2) the grantor cannot have reserved a power to recall the deed from the escrow agent. If either of these conditions are not met, there can be no relation back. Title will pass only when the deed is delivered to the grantee.

7. **Warranties of Title** - There are three types of deeds distinguished by the warranties the grantor makes as to the quality of the title conveyed. A *general warranty deed* warrants title against all defects whether they arose before or after the grantor took title. A *special warranty deed* on the other hand warrants only that the grantor has not caused the title defect. The grantor of a special warranty deed is not liable for a title defect that arose before the grantor took title. A *quitclaim deed* makes no warranties of any kind with regard to title quality.

   a. **The Standard Title Covenants** - In a general warranty deed, the grantor warrants or covenants that:

      1) The grantor owns the interest in land the deed purports to convey (a warranty known as the *covenant of seisin*);

2) The grantor has the power to convey that interest (a warranty known as the *covenant of a right to convey*);

3) The grantor's title is not encumbered by a mortgage, lien, easement, covenant or other interest (a warranty known as the *covenant against encumbrances*);

4) The grantee's possession will not be disturbed by a lawful claimant (a warranty known as the *covenant of quiet enjoyment*);

5) The grantor will defend the grantee from such claims (a warranty known as the *covenant of general warranty*); and

6) The grantor will perform any acts, such as the execution of additional documents, reasonably necessary to perfect the title the deed purports to convey (a warranty known as the *covenant of further assurances*).

The first three covenants listed above are known as *present covenants.* They are breached, if at all, at the time the grantor delivers the deed to the grantee. In the majority of jurisdictions, the present covenants do not run with the land so as to benefit a remote grantee.

The second three covenants listed above are known as *future covenants*. They are breached when the grantee's possession is disturbed by one with paramount title. These covenants are generally held to run with the land so as to benefit remote grantees.

b. **Damages** - Damages for breach of one of the title covenants is limited to the amount the grantor received when he or she sold the property. This limitation holds even if the land markedly increases in value.

8. **Merger by Deed** - Once a deed has been delivered and accepted, any promise in the contract of sale related to title quality merges into the deed. Thus, a suit cannot be maintained on the implied warranty in a contract of sale that the seller has marketable title once the buyer has accepted the seller's deed. The buyer must look to the warranties in the deed, if any, to pursue an action against the seller.

Example: A enters into a written contract to sell Blackacre to B and promises to deliver marketable title. At closing, B accepts a special warranty deed. Two years later, a mining company established that it holds a profit in the coal underneath Blackacre which was conveyed to the company before A acquired an interest in the property. The company starts strip mining the coal. B has no cause of action against A. A's promise to deliver marketable title merged into the special warranty deed. A did not breach any covenant in a special warranty deed.

9. **Estoppel by Deed** - A person may sign and deliver a deed to land that the person does not own. If the grantee received a warranty deed, the grantee can sue the grantor for damages. If the grantor later acquires the interest the deed purported to convey, the grantee has additional rights. The grantor of a deed is generally estopped to deny the language in the deed that purported to convey the interest. As a result, when the grantor later acquires the interest, it inures automatically to the grantee of the deed.

   Example: A gives a deed to Blackacre to B. Blackacre is in fact owned by A's uncle of the same name. Shortly after closing, A's uncle dies leaving Blackacre to A. When A acquires title, it will pass immediately to B under the doctrine of estoppel by deed.

C. MORTGAGES

The buyer usually requires financing to purchase property today. Typically, the buyer gives a mortgage to a lender on the security of the property the buyer will acquire. The buyer or borrower in the mortgage transaction is the *mortgagor*. The lender is the *mortgagee*. Not all mortgages, of course, are loans made to enable a purchase. Any person with an alienable interest in land can mortgage that interest.

1. **Lien or Title Theory** - Historically, a mortgage was secured through the actual transfer of *title* to the mortgagee. Today, in the vast majority of states, the mortgagee acquires a *lien* on the property, not title. A lien is the right to look to the property to satisfy the obligation secured by the mortgage. A few states still hold to the title theory. A few others take an intermediate position whereby they apply the lien theory until closing and the title theory afterwards. Today, there is little practical difference between the lien theory, title theory and intermediate theory states in the enforcement of a mortgage. As noted earlier, there is some authority that a mortgage by one joint tenant severs the tenancy in a title theory state but not in jurisdictions that follow the other theories.

2. **The Equity of Redemption** - At common law, mortgages usually took the form of a conveyance by the borrower to the lender of a fee simple on condition subsequent. The borrower retained a power to terminate the fee if the mortgage loan was repaid on a stated due date. The due date was called "law day" because on that date the lender would acquire a fee simple absolute if the borrower had not paid. Over the centuries, equity intervened and permitted borrowers to pay late. The borrower's right to pay late and redeem the property came to be known as the mortgagor's *equity of redemption.*

3. **Foreclosure** - Eventually, the lenders sought relief from the courts of equity. They obtained court orders that required debtors to pay by a date decreed by the court or be forever barred from redeeming their property. These orders *foreclosed* the debtor's equity of redemption. At common law, the mortgagee acquired the property in fee simple on foreclosure, a type of foreclosure known as *strict foreclosure.* Today, almost all foreclosures are done by sale.

   a. **Foreclosure Sales** - Foreclosure sales are conducted either through a judicial proceeding known as a foreclosure action or under a *power of sale*. Powers of sale are established in a type of mortgage known as a *deed of trust*. In this type of mortgage transaction, the mortgagor conveys title to the mortgaged property to a trustee who is given authority to sell the property in the event of default. The rights of the parties to the sales proceeds do not differ if a foreclosure sale is carried out by judicial action or under a power of sale.

The proceeds of a foreclosure sale are applied first, to satisfy court costs and other expenses of foreclosure, second, to pay the mortgage debt, and third, to satisfy any junior liens. Mortgages, liens and other interests generally rank in priority of time. An unrecorded interest, however, may be subordinated to a later one under the recording statutes.

If a foreclosure sale does not fetch the amount of the mortgage debt, the mortgagor remains liable for the *deficiency*. The liability is personal and is generally dischargeable in bankruptcy. Conversely, the mortgagor is entitled to any *surplus* from the sales proceeds if they exceed the amount of the mortgage debt, foreclosure expenses, and other liens entitled to be paid.

b. **Title Acquired at Foreclosure** - The purchaser at a foreclosure sale acquires title free of the mortgage lien foreclosed upon and also free of any liens which are subordinate to the lien foreclosed upon. The purchaser takes subject to any senior liens and any statutory right of redemption in the mortgagor.

Omitted Parties – Foreclosure proceedings do not affect the rights of any party who is omitted from the proceeding. If the omitted party is the mortgagor of the interest foreclosed upon, the mortgagor can exercise the equitable right of redemption by paying the purchaser the amount of the mortgage debt. If the omitted party is a junior lien holder, the lien holder can redeem in the same manner, by paying the purchaser the amount of the debt foreclosed upon. The omitted junior lien holder can also foreclose but in any such foreclosure proceeding the senior mortgage will have priority.

Deed In Lieu of Foreclosure – A mortgagee may agree to accept the mortgagor's fee title instead of foreclosing. Such an agreement avoids the expense and difficulty of foreclosure for the mortgagee. It relieves the mortgagor of any liability for a deficiency. A mortgagee who accepts a deed in lieu of foreclosure takes the title subject to any junior liens the mortgagee placed on the property. To extinguish these, the mortgagee must foreclose.

4. **Statutory Redemption** - By statute, in roughly half the states, the mortgagor is given a statutory right of redemption, distinct from the equitable right of redemption discussed above. Upon payment of the amount obtained at the foreclosure sale, plus interest, the mortgagor can redeem the property from the purchaser who acquired it at the foreclosure. The statutes vary a great deal particularly as to how long the mortgagor has to redeem the property.

5. **Typical Mortgage Clauses** - Mortgages typically set forth acceleration and due on sale clauses.

   a. *Acceleration Clauses* - An acceleration clause allows any creditor of an indebtedness payable in installments to collect the entire amount of the debt in the event of default, not just the amount of any overdue installments.

   b. *Due on Sale Clauses* - A due on sale clause makes a mortgage payable if the mortgagor sells the property that secures the mortgage. Many state courts had ruled due on sale clauses were restraints on alienation. Today, such clauses are enforceable by federal law.

   c. If there is no due on sale clause, the mortgagor can sell the property in one of two ways: (1) where the buyer takes the property *"subject to"* the mortgage; or (2) where the buyer *"assumes"* the mortgage. When the buyer assumes the mortgage, the buyer becomes personally liable to the mortgagee for the amount of the mortgage debt. When the buyer takes subject to mortgage, on the other hand, the buyer is not personally liable to the mortgagee. In the event of default, the mortgagee can foreclose on the mortgage and recover possession of the property, but cannot collect the debt personally from the buyer.

   d. Note the original mortgagor remains liable to the mortgagee whether the buyer assumes or takes subject to the mortgage. The original mortgagor stands as a *surety*. If the original mortgagor pays the mortgage debt, the mortgagor will be *subrogated* to the rights of the mortgagee. These rights would include the right to foreclose on the mortgage lien.

   Example: A borrows money from B to buy a house. A gives B a mortgage on the property to secure the loan. A later sells the house to C. The contract between A and C specifies that C assumes the mortgage. C defaults. At this point, B can sue either A or C. C assumed the mortgage and is personally liable on the mortgage debt. A continues to be liable on his original undertaking. If B sues A and recovers the full amount of the debt, A is subrogated to B's rights. These rights would include the mortgage lien, and A could file a foreclosure action.

6. **Installment Land Sale Contracts and Equitable Mortgages** - A buyer of land may agree to pay the purchase price in installments, with the seller retaining legal title to the property until all the installments are paid. In the event of default the seller may be able to retain the installments paid in addition to recovering possession. Today, most jurisdictions by statute or judicial decision give buyers in installment land sale contracts rights similar to those enjoyed by mortgagors. Courts have long looked behind the form of a transaction if necessary to protect borrowers from a forfeiture. They will treat a transaction as an *equitable mortgage* if the transaction poses a similar risk.

Example: A needed funds. B agreed to loan him the funds if A gave B a deed to A's farm, Blackacre. B then leased the farm to A under a written lease agreement. This transaction has many features of a mortgage and puts A at risk. B could evict A if A defaulted in the rent payments. A would lose any payments made through the date of default and Blackacre. Courts have treated such sale-leaseback transactions as mortgages under the equitable mortgage doctrine.

7. **Absolute Deed Intended As Security** – The desire to protect a mortgagee from forfeiture had led the courts to fashion an exception to the parol evidence rule. The courts will receive parol evidence to show that the grantee of an absolute deed took the deed as security for a loan. The absolute deed will then be treated as a mortgage.

8. **The Secondary Mortgage Market** – Mortgagees often sell their interests today in the secondary mortgage market. In any assignment of the mortgagee's interest, the mortgagee must negotiate the mortgage note to the assignee. The mortgage lien follows the note. With a proper negotiation, the assignee acquires the rights of a holder under the law of negotiable instruments. These rights may include the rights of a holder in due course.

   Example: A's small business is in need of financing. A borrows from Town Bank and gives the Bank a mortgage on his home. The Town Bank loan officer assures A that Town Bank will look to the assets of A's business before foreclosing on the home mortgage. Town Bank then assigns the mortgage and negotiates the mortgage note to City Bank. As a result, City Bank holds the mortgage lien. It is also likely that City Bank is a holder in due course and can enforce the mortgage free of A's claim that the Bank should look to his business assets first. A holder in due course takes free of virtually all claims and defenses to pay the obligation evinced by a note.

D. CONVEYANCE BY WILL

Very often real property is transferred through a decedent's estate in accordance with the provisions of a Will. Wills speak from the moment of the testator's death. People draft Wills, however, when they are alive. Sometimes changes occur between the drafting of a Will and the testator's death that make it impossible to distribute real property through an estate as directed by the Will.

1. **Lapse** – A devise may fail because the named devisee predeceased the testator. The courts at common law ruled such a devise "lapsed" and could not be carried out. Today, virtually all states have adopted anti-lapse statutes that provide an alternative taker to the predeceased devisee. The anti-lapse statutes generally provide that the property will pass to any living issue of the devisee named in the Will. If the devisee has no living issue, the statutes vary as to how many other alternatives they provide. All the anti-lapse statutes, however, direct that the testator's intent will govern the application of the statute.

Example: A dies leaving a Will that states, "I devise Blackacre to my brother, B, and if he does not survive me, to my sister, C." B predeceased A, leaving a daughter, D. All the anti-lapse statutes will respect A's expressed intent and C will take Blackacre rather than D. If A's Will had stated "I devise Blackacre to B, if he survives me," most jurisdictions would hold the devise lapsed when B predeceased A. Again, this result would be based on the testator's intent expressed in the language of the Will conditioning the devise on survivorship.

2. **Ademption** – A similar problem arises if the testator no longer owns property at the time of his or her death that the language of the testator's Will purports to devise. At common law, the courts would not enforce the devise on the theory that the testator had adeemed (law Latin for "had taken away") the property. Most jurisdictions still follow this approach if the devise names specific property. Ademption does not apply to general devises. Faced with a specific devise, the courts will adeem the grant and will generally not receive extrinsic evidence that the testator had a contrary intent.

   Example: A died leaving a Will that purported to devise his "Palm Beach vacation home to B and her heirs." A had sold the home two years before her death and bought a condominium in Naples. Most courts would hold the devise was adeemed. The will named a specific property. Most courts would not allow evidence that A had intended B to have any vacation home she owned at her death. Note, however, a general devise, "all my real property," would not be adeemed. Sometimes even a specific devise can be saved from ademption through construction of the Will. If A's Will had simply stated, for example, that she devised "her vacation home to B" a court could construe this language to cover the vacation home A owned at her death, the Naples condominium.

3. **Exoneration** – The difference between a specific and a general devise was also important in the traditional doctrine of exoneration. If a testator had mortgaged real property specifically devised in his or her Will, the English courts ruled the mortgage would be paid or "exonerated" from the residual estate. This rule has generally been changed by statutes like the Uniform Probate Code. Under modern statutes, the devisee takes the property subject to the mortgage.

   Example: A's Will devised "Blackacre to my son, B and his heirs, with all the rest, residue and remainder of my estate to my daughter, C and her heirs." When A died, Blackacre had a fair market value of $50,000 but was subject to a mortgage of $20,000. He also held stocks, bonds and a bank account worth $30,000. Under the traditional rule, Blackacre would be distributed to B free of the mortgage. C would get $10,000 through the residuary clause, as the remaining funds would have been used to exonerate Blackacre. Under modern statutes, like the Uniform Probate Code, B would receive Blackacre subject to the mortgage lien and C would receive the $30,000 in stocks, bonds and cash.

E. FRAUDULENT CONVEYANCES

Creditors may set aside a conveyance of real property made to avoid their claims. A creditor can reach property fraudulently conveyed in the hand of the grantee. There are two ways to establish a fraudulent conveyance. The first method is based on proving the fraudulent intent of the grantor. The second method is based on more objective criteria.

1. **Intent** – A creditor can set aside a fraudulent conveyance if the creditor proves the debtor transferred property to another with the intent to evade the creditor's claim. Because an evasive purpose is difficult to prove, the courts presumed certain acts were done with fraudulent intent. These acts are called "badges of fraud" and include:

    a. the transfer of the property to a relative or other insider;
    b. the transfer of title to property the debtor continues to use and control;
    c. efforts to conceal the transfer or remove or hide other assets; or
    d. the transfer of property shortly after a lawsuit against the debtor was filed or threatened.

2. **Objective Criteria** – Modern fraudulent conveyance statutes also allow a creditor to avoid a transfer that was made while the debtor was *insolvent* and for which the debtor received less than *reasonably equivalent value*. A debtor is deemed "insolvent" under these statutes if the debtor's liabilities exceed his or her assets or if the debtor is not paying his or her debts as they become due. Intention is irrelevant in a challenge under the objective tests provided by these statutes.

    Example: A owns Blackacre which is worth $50,000. She has no other substantial assets. A's debts exceed $100,000 at the time she gives B a deed to Blackacre. Any one of A's creditors can attach Blackacre in B's hands because he received it through a fraudulent conveyance. The transfer to B occurred when A was insolvent and A did not receive equivalent value for the property. As such, the transfer is deemed a fraudulent conveyance without regard to A's intent to evade the creditor.

X. GOOD FAITH PURCHASERS AND THE RECORDING SYSTEM

The courts at common law applied the rule of "first in time, first in right" to determine priority among competing property interests. The rule could be harsh on a purchaser of property who had no notice of prior interest. As a result, all fifty states have enacted recording systems which allow public recordation of interests in property. Statutes also protect good faith purchasers of property from earlier, unrecorded interests.

A. TYPES OF RECORDING ACTS

There are three types of recording statutes designed to protect purchasers of property. Only two of these are in wide use with respect to real property.

1. **Race Statutes** - A race statute protects a purchaser from an earlier interest if the purchaser records his or her interest first. The winner of the race to the recorder of deeds office enjoys priority of title. A race statute encourages prompt recording. Race statutes are not common in American law.

   Example: A gives a mortgage to his friend, B, as security for a loan. B does not immediately record her interest. C later loans A money taking a mortgage on the same property. A tells C of B's mortgage before C advances any sums to A. Nevertheless, C proceeds with the transaction and promptly records his mortgage. B then records her mortgage. Under a race statute, C would have priority over B. C's knowledge of B's interest is irrelevant under such a statute.

2. **Notice Statutes** - A notice statute protects a purchaser from an earlier interest only if the purchaser has no notice of the interest, through the record or otherwise. Roughly half the states have notice statutes.

3. **Race-Notice Statutes** - A race-notice statute protects a purchaser from an earlier interest only if the purchaser has no notice of the interest ***and*** the purchaser records before the holder of the prior interest. Roughly half the states employ race-notice statutes.

   Example: A conveys Blackacre to B on July 1. B does not immediately record his deed. A then sells Blackacre to C on July 15. C has no notice of B's interest at the time of his purchase. B records his deed on July 20. C records on July 21. In a suit between B and C in a state which has adopted a notice statute, C would win. C did not have any notice of B's interest at the time C purchased. In a race-notice jurisdiction, however, C would lose to B. A race-notice statute would not protect C because C did not record before B.

B. INTERESTS NOT COVERED BY THE RECORDING ACTS

The recording acts protect a purchaser from prior interests not disclosed in the record. The acts, however, do not cover all interests in property.

1. **Interests Arising by Operation of Law** - As we have seen, interests in property may arise by operation of law. Persons can acquire property rights by adverse possession, prescription, and necessity. Interests of this nature do not arise through a deed or other recordable instrument. The recording acts are generally held not to apply to them, and a good faith purchaser takes subject to them.

2. **Statutory and Judicial Liens** - Statutes confer property rights. Unpaid contractors and suppliers can obtain mechanics' liens on property. A mechanics lien, once it is perfected, can relate back to the time the contractor's or supplier's right to payment arose. The recording acts generally do not protect purchasers from these liens.

   Judgment creditors may obtain such liens by the entry of judgment or by attachments. These judicial liens are usually deemed to lie outside the recording acts. Purchasers need to check the judgment indexes.

3. **Short Term Leases** - Short term leases, from one to three years, are generally not recorded. Most recording acts do not protect a purchaser from such leases.

C. PURCHASERS PROTECTED BY THE RECORDING ACTS

The recording statutes generally protect good faith purchasers who give valuable consideration for property. Others are not necessarily protected by the acts and may acquire property subject to prior unrecorded interests.

1. **Donees** - Heirs, devisees, donees and others who do not give value for property are not protected by the acts.

2. **Judgment Lien Creditors** - Persons who acquire liens by entry of judgment or attachment are usually not deemed to be purchasers under the recording acts absent express statutory language bringing them within the protection of the acts.

3. **Mortgagees** - A person who acquires a mortgage for a pre-existing debt has been denied the protection of the recording act. Courts reaching this result rely on the pre-existing duty rule and reason that such a mortgagee has not given a valuable consideration. A revision of the interest rate, an extension of the time of payment or other change in the term of the indebtedness would constitute consideration and presumably give the mortgagee the protection of the act.

4. **Mechanic's Lien Holders** - Most states allow persons who have improved property through their labor or materials to place a lien on that property if they are not paid. Such lien holders are usually denied the protection of the acts on the theory discussed above. They have not given new value for the lien they acquire by operation of law.

5. **Purchasers Who Have Made An Executory Promise To Pay** - A purchaser who has promised to pay for land but has not yet paid the agreed price is not deemed to have given value and falls outside the protection of the recording act. If the promise to pay is embodied in a negotiable instrument, however, the courts hold the purchaser has given value. They reason that the instrument could be negotiated to a holder in due course.

6. **Purchasers Who Have Paid Only A Nominal Consideration** - Under the majority view, payment of a nominal consideration, i.e., "One dollar, In Hand Paid," will not bring a purchaser within the protection of the recording acts. Neither will a recital of "love and affection" or similar expression of non-pecuniary consideration.

D. THE SHELTER PRINCIPLE

Any transferee of property acquires all the rights of his or her transferor. A good faith purchaser for value may sell, give, devise or otherwise transfer his or her rights. The person acquiring those rights takes shelter in the good faith purchaser's title and need not establish good faith purchaser status in their own right to enjoy the protection of the recording act. **Example:** Blackacre was encumbered by an unrecorded mortgage when it was purchased by A for a valuable consideration. A had no notice of the mortgage at the time of the purchase. A devised Blackacre to B. Sometime later, the mortgagee attempted to foreclose on the mortgage. B can defend under the recording act even though he is not a "purchaser" in his own right. A was a good faith purchaser. A devised his rights to B. B can take shelter in A's title to defeat the mortgagee. The same result would follow if B was purchaser who knew of the mortgagee's interest when he purchased Blackacre from A. A transferee of a good faith purchaser enjoys those rights derivatively.

The shelter principle cannot be used to "launder" title. A person holding title to land who is aware of an unrecorded interest cannot sell the land to a good faith purchaser and then reacquire it to defeat the interest.

E. NOTICE

Race-notice and notice statutes protect purchasers who have no notice of a prior interest. Notice can be *actual* or *constructive*. There are two types of constructive notice that will remove a person from the protection of the recording acts, *record notice* and *inquiry notice*.

1. **Actual Notice** - A person with actual knowledge or notice of a prior unrecorded interest will not take free of that interest under either a notice or a race-notice recording act.

   Example: B is interested in purchasing Blackacre. While A is showing B the property he tells B that C has the right to remove timber from the estate. C's profit in the timber is unrecorded. B later purchases the property. B cannot prevent C from logging Blackacre on the basis of a race-notice or notice recording act. B had actual notice of C's interest.

2. **Inquiry Notice** - A purchaser may have knowledge of facts that require further investigation as to the status of a prior interest. If the purchaser fails to undertake that investigation, the courts will hold the purchaser to the knowledge further inquiry would have revealed.

   a. **Visual Inspection** - The courts generally charge a purchaser with a duty to inquire about interests that are apparent on a visual inspection of the property.

      Example: A purchased Blackacre from B. A drive bisects Blackacre and leads to C's garage. A has inquiry notice of C's easement and will take Blackacre subject to the easement even if it is unrecorded.

   b. **Claims of Parties In Possession** - A purchaser is generally charged with a duty to inquire about the rights of parties in actual possession of the land, including tenants.

      Example: A purchased Blackacre from B, the record owner. C lived in a cabin on Blackacre and had posted "No Trespassing" signs. A will be charged with inquiry notice of any interest C had in the land. ***Wineberg v. Moore***, 194 F.Supp. 12 (N.D.Cal. 1961).

   c. **Recitals in Title Documents** - A deed or other title document may refer to an unrecorded interest. The courts may charge a purchaser with a duty to investigate such a reference.

Example: A purchased Blackacre from B. A deed in B's chain of title refers to "the mortgage to First Bank of even date herewith." The mortgage does not appear of record. Nevertheless, the courts would likely hold that A should ask First Bank about the mortgage. Failure to do so will result in A being charged with inquiry notice of the encumbrance.

Courts have charged purchasers with inquiry notice of prior interests on the basis of recitals in deeds that are quite difficult to track down. As a result, a few states have adopted statutes that impute inquiry notice to a title examiner only if the interest referred to in the recital is itself recorded.

d. **Quitclaim Deeds** - Most jurisdictions hold that a grantee under a quitclaim deed has no greater duty of investigation than any other grantee. In a minority of jurisdictions, however, they are charged with a greater duty, and in a few states, are deemed to have inquiry notice of all unrecorded encumbrances.

3. **Record Notice** - The courts charge a purchaser with constructive notice of prior interests that are revealed in recorded documents in the purchaser's *chain of title*. The phrase, "chain of title," means the documents recorded by the purchaser's predecessor in interest to the property which can be found thorough a standard title examination of the public records.

F. TITLE EXAMINATION

A title examiner can only find records through the index maintained by the recorder of deeds. There are two types of index in wide use today.

1. **Tract Index -** With a tract index, title documents are organized by a street address or other reference to specific properties. Every deed, mortgage, and other document that affects title to a tract are listed together under the reference to that tract. A tract index eliminates many "chain of title" problems but they are not as prevalent as grantor-grantee indexes.

2. **Grantor-Grantee Index -** With a grantor-grantee index, the title documents are organized by reference to the names of the parties to each transaction. A title examiner for a buyer of property would begin with the seller's name in the grantee index looking for all transactions that involved the seller as grantee. Working back, the examiner would find the name of the seller's predecessor in title. The examiner would run that name through the grantee index to find that person's predecessor. The process would be repeated until the examiner reached an acceptable root of title, such as a land patent from the United States. The examiner would then run all the names the examination had revealed through the grantor indexes. In this way, the examiner would find any grants, mortgages, or conveyance from anyone in the chain of title.

   Example: Edwards is planning to buy Blackacre from Davis. The examiner runs Davis's name through the grantee index and finds Davis acquired the property by deed from Charles in 1971. The examiner then runs Charles's name through the same index and finds Charles acquired the land from Baxter in 1952. Repeating the process, the examiner finds Baxter acquired the land from Able in 1930. Able acquired the property in 1890 which is as far as the examiner and local practice deem necessary. The examiner will then take Able's name through the grantor index until 1930 looking for any conveyances Able may have made. The examiner will run Baxter's name through the grantor index up to 1952, and so on. By this method, the examiner would find a mortgage, for example, given by Charles to First National Bank in 1988.

3. **Related Indexes** - A title examination will require a search of tax liens, mechanics liens, and judgment indexes if they are indexed separately from title documents. The examiner should also review the probate, marriage, and divorce records indexed under the name of every grantor and grantee in the chain of title. The examiner should make sure the seller is not a debtor in bankruptcy proceedings.

G. CHAIN OF TITLE PROBLEMS

The nature of the indexes, particularly the grantor-grantee index, causes some documents that were actually recorded to be impossible to find in a standard title search.

1. **Wild Deeds** - A document may be filed with the recorder of deeds but be unconnected with a purchaser's chain of title. The majority of jurisdictions hold such a wild deed does not impart record notice to purchaser.

   Example: A conveys Blackacre to B, who does not record his deed. B then conveys Blackacre to C who does record her deed. Her deed is indexed under B's name as grantor and C's name as grantee. A then conveys Blackacre to D. D records. In the majority of jurisdictions, D will not be charged with notice of C's deed even though it was recorded. C's deed was wild. D's title examiner will begin the title search with A's name in the grantee index. The examiner will go back to a root of title and run the names forward. in the grantor index. The examiner will not find the deed from A to B because B did not record. As a result, the title examiner will never encounter C's name let alone the deed from B to C. The examiner will be looking for documents from A as grantor and will not find the B to C deed.

2. **Deeds Out From A Common Grantor** - A purchaser may be charged with notice of restrictions in the deeds to adjacent parcels if the parcels were once commonly owned with the land purchased.

   Example: A owns Blackacre and subdivides it into twelve building lots. A sells ten lots with restrictive covenants in the deed limiting use of the lots to single family dwellings. A covenants in each of the ten deeds that he will restrict the use of the land he retains to single family dwellings as well. When A cannot sell the last two lots, he sells one to B without restrictions. In roughly half the states that have addressed the issue, B will be charged with notice of the restrictions in the deeds to his neighbor's lots even though they lay outside the chain of title to his lot. Other states do not charge B with notice.

States that do not charge a purchaser with record notice of restrictions in deeds out from a common grantor may charge the purchaser with *inquiry notice* of the same restrictions. A purchaser is charged with inquiry notice of restrictions that are evident through a visual inspection of the property. A person who buys a lot in a residential subdivision could be expected to inquire further if the person plans to operate a business on the lot. The neighborhood scheme may give rise to a duty to investigate further as to any restrictions even if the seller proposes to sell an unrestricted deed to the purchaser.

3. **Deeds Recorded Early** - A deed may be unconnected to a purchaser's chain of title because it is recorded too early to be found in the standard title search.

   Example: A owns Blackacre in fee simple absolute. A's nephew, B, however, claims to be the owner when he gives a mortgage on the property to C. C records the mortgage. A then dies devising Blackacre to B. Under the doctrine of estoppel by deed, discussed earlier, C's mortgage would now automatically attach to B's interest in Blackacre. B, however, immediately sells Blackacre to D and does not remit any portion of the sales proceeds to C. B then defaults on C's loan. In most states, C cannot foreclose on Blackacre. D would be protected by the recording act because D would not find C's mortgage in a standard title search. When the title examiner runs through the grantor indexes, he will be looking for conveyances out from A during the time C's mortgage was recorded. The mortgage was thus recorded "too early" to be found in a standard title examination using the grantor-grantee indexes.

4. **Deeds Recorded Late** - Deeds can also be recorded too late to be found in the standard title search. As with deeds recorded too early, the majority rule holds they do not impart record notice.

   Example: A gives his daughter, B, a deed to Blackacre. B does not record the deed. A then gives a deed to Blackacre to his son, C, who knows of the previous deed A gave B. C records. B then hurriedly records her deed. C sells Blackacre to D, a purchaser for value who has no actual knowledge of any of the foregoing events. A title examination on D's behalf will not reveal B's deed even though it is recorded. When the examiner runs through the grantor indexes, the examiner will not look for deeds out from A recorded after the deed to C. B recorded "too late" and as a result her deed will not be found in a standard title examination using the grantor-grantee indexes.

H. PROBLEMS CAUSED BY THE RECORDER

The decent people who work in the recorder of deeds office make mistakes. Jurisdictions differ over the consequences of those mistakes.

1. **Unacknowledged Deeds** - A deed will transfer title between the grantor and grantee even though it is not acknowledged before a notary. Most jurisdictions, however, require a notarized acknowledgement before a deed can be recorded. If the recorder inadvertently accepts an unacknowledged deed, the majority rule is that deed is not properly recorded and does not impart record notice. More troubling cases hold that an improperly acknowledged deed also does not impart record notice.

Example: A gives B a signed deed to Blackacre. The deed, however, was not signed before a notary. B persuades a notary to affix her seal and attestation to the deed. The deed, of course, should have been acknowledged in the notary's presence. B then records the deed. A then sells to D. D's title examiner will find the deed from A to B. D can claim, however, if he proves the stated facts that B's deed was not properly recorded because of the defective acknowledgement. The better reasoned cases would charge D with notice of B's interest but there are cases to the contrary. An examiner can see a missing acknowledgment but has no way of knowing from the record of many defective acknowledgments.

2. **Mis-indexing** - The recorder may mistakenly index a document or fail, through an oversight, to index it at all. There is a split of authority over who bears the risk of such mistakes. The majority of jurisdictions hold that a document is legally "recorded" when it is presented to the recorder with the proper fee. A sizable minority holds such a document cannot be found in a standard title search and should not defeat a good faith purchaser. These latter authorities maintain the person who presented the document for recording should have verified it had been properly recorded.

   Under either view, the party injured by the recorder's mistake can sue the recorder. The office bonds against these mistakes.

I. REFORMS

The problems associated with the recording systems have led many jurisdictions to enact reforms.

1. **Registration of Title ("Torrens Systems")** - Several states have authorized counties to adopt a system of registering land titles. In a title registration or Torrens System, a landowner brings an action to adjudicate title. The court determines that the plaintiff has title subject to any mortgage or other encumbrance found to exist. The court then enters judgment on the title extinguishing all other claims. The title as adjudicated is then registered on a certificate of title. Subsequent transfers of the land are based on the title certificate in much the same way as is done with automobiles. The buyer of a registered title will have a new certificate issued in the buyer's name reflecting anything that has happened to the title since the seller's certificate was issued. The buyer's mortgage would be noted on the new certificate, for example.

2. **Tract Indexes** - Many locales have moved to a tract index from a grantor-grantee index. A tract index eliminates the wild deed, late recorded deed and early recorded deed problems outlined above. It also eliminates problems associated with the spelling of names.

3. **Marketable Title Acts** – Finally, many states have adopted marketable title acts. A.marketable title act is designed to limit searches as much as possible to a limited period. The Uniform Marketable Title Act, for example, gives marketable title, free of any adverse claims, to any person who has an unbroken chain of title of record for thirty years or more.

XI. EMINENT DOMAIN AND INVERSE CONDEMNATION

The federal and state governments have the inherent power to acquire private property for public use. This sovereign authority is called the power of *eminent domain* and the government's act of appropriating the property is called *condemnation*. Federal and state constitutions require that when "private property" is "taken" for "public use" the owner must receive "just compensation."

A. PRIVATE PROPERTY

Generally any interest in property may be taken by eminent domain. Cases have compensated owner for loss of air rights, riparian rights, and the right to receive interest on funds, for example. The interest in property need not be possessory in order to give rise to a claim it has been unconstitutionally taken.

Example: A county builds an airport near Blackacre. Aircraft taking off and landing fly directly over Blackacre at low altitude. The government's action may be challenged as a taking of the owner's interest in the air above Blackacre. *Griggs v. Allegheny County*, 369 U.S. 84 (1962).

B. PUBLIC USE

Constitutional phrases like "public use" or "public purpose" do not limit the taking power to instances where the government will actually appropriate the property for its own use or the public's. If the taking serves a legitimate public purpose, it will be upheld even though the government will not hold the property but will distribute it to other individuals.

Example: A state government determines that land ownership in the state is too concentrated. It takes Blackacre in order to distribute it to the tenants who work the estate. It pays just compensation to the owner of Blackacre. The state had such a power under the law of eminent domain. The phrase, "public use" in the Fifth Amendment does not prevent the state from taking the action. ***Hawaii Housing Authority v. Midkiff***, 467 U.S. 229 (1984).

As part of a comprehensive plan to foster economic development, a city may condemn properties that are not blighted and then transfer the properties to a developer for the construction of a hotel, shopping center and other privately owned uses. In assessing whether a condemnation serves a "public use," the federal constitution only requires that a public purpose be served by the taking. In general, the federal courts should defer to judgment of state and local officials that an exercise of eminent domain serves a public purpose unless it appears to be a pre textual justification for transferring property from one private landowner to another. ***Kelo v. City of New London***, 125 S. Ct. 2655; 162 L. Ed. 2d 439 (2005).

C. JUST COMPENSATION

When property is taken the owner is generally entitled to the fair market value of the interest at the time of the taking as determined by a trier of fact. If part of a parcel of land is taken, the owner may be entitled to severance damages for a resulting loss in value of the part not taken. If the government takes land that is not held in fee simple, the condemnation award should be apportioned among the present and future interest holders. Tenants are generally entitled to compensation when a leasehold is taken by eminent domain or inverse condemnation.

D. TAKING

In building roads and other public improvements, governments take property directly through formal condemnation proceedings. The right to compensation may arise, however, if the government impairs the value of a property interest indirectly, a so called *inverse condemnation*. Government regulation may unconstitutionally impinge on rights to property and amount to a compensable taking.

1. **Balancing Test** – In most cases where a regulation is challenged, the courts apply a three part test to determine whether the regulation has gone "too far" so that it can be challenged as a taking. The courts will examine: (1) the nature of the governmental action; (2) the economic impact of the regulation on the property owner; and (3) the extent to which the regulation interfered with distinct "investment backed" expectations. ***Penn Central Transp. Co. v. New York City***, 438 U.S. 104, 124 (1978).

   a. **Noxious Uses** – In applying the three part test, the courts are likely to uphold a regulation designed to abate a use of property that threatens the health and safety of the public. No property owner has the right to maintain a nuisance, so government regulation designed to abate a nuisance does not constitute a taking of "property."

   b. **Reciprocity of Advantage** – Courts tend to uphold governmental action that results in costs and benefits that are widely shared. Land burdened by regulation often benefits from a similar burden placed on neighboring parcels. For example, a zoning regulation that limits the use of a lot to residential purposes benefits from having the residential character of the neighborhood preserved by the regulation's restriction on neighboring lots. The courts are generally unwilling to find an unconstitutional taking when a regulation engenders such a "reciprocity of advantage."

   c. **Individualized Determinations** – On the other hand, if governmental action is focused on a specific property owner, the courts scrutinize the action more carefully.

   Example: A property owner applies for a municipal building permit in order to enlarge her store. The city agrees to grant the permit if the owner would dedicate a portion of her property to the public as open green space and a bike path. The city contends the green space will alleviate the risk of flooding caused by the larger store's bigger parking lot. The city also contends the bike path will alleviate traffic caused in part by the store's customers. The court found the conditions imposed by the city were a taking. The city had to show an essential nexus between the impact of the larger store and the conditions the city imposed on the landowner. The city's conclusory allegations about the risk of flooding and burden of increased traffic would not suffice to show the dedication was necessary. ***Dolan v. City of Tigard,*** 512 U.S. 374 (1994).

d. **Temporary Taking** - The United States Supreme Court has permitted a state agency to place a moratorium on development of an environmentally threatened area without considering the moratorium to be a taking. The Court applied the balancing test and considered the limited duration of the ban as one factor in weighing the constitutionality of the moratorium. ***Tahoe-Sierra Preservation Council, Inc. v. Tahoe Regional Planning Agency***, 535 U.S. 302 (2002).

2. **Takings "Per Se"** – The courts do not apply a balancing test to governmental actions that have either one of the following effects:

a. Physical Invasion - If the governmental action is a physical invasion of a landowner's property, the courts will consider the action a taking *per se*. The courts consider the right to exclude others as central to property ownership.

Example: A local government requires homeowners to permit a cable television company to run wire across their property. The action is a taking even though there is little interference with the owners' use and enjoyment of their properties. ***Loretto v. Teleprompter Manhattan CATV Corp.***, 458 U.S. 419 (1982).

b. Loss of All Economically Viable Use - The courts will find a taking *per se* if the governmental action has deprived a property owner of substantially all the economic value of the property.

Example: An individual purchased a beach front lot for a substantial sum of money in order to build a vacation home. The state later bans all building on the beach which eliminates nearly all the economic value of the lot. The United States Supreme Court ruled the state's ban was a taking per se without considering the government's interest in preserving the beach. ***Lucas v. South Carolina Coastal Council***, 505 U.S. 1003 (1992).

XII. CONTROL OF LAND USE THROUGH ZONING

A state has the power to regulate the use of land through the exercise of its police power, i.e., its authority to promote the health, safety and well-being of the people.

A. ENABLING ACT

The state generally delegates its authority to regulate land use to local governments. The state statute that authorizes cities and counties to adopt zoning regulations is both the source and the principal limitation of a local government's power. A local government cannot regulate land use except as provided in the state enabling act.

Example: An amusement park remains open for business after midnight. The ensuing disruption leads the local township to adopt a zoning ordinance that limits the hours of operation of amusement parks. The Enabling Act, however, authorized the township to regulate types of uses not the hours of operation of a commercial enterprise. Therefore, the ordinance was invalid. ***Bainbridge Township v. Funtime, Inc.***, 55 Oh.St.3d 106 (1990). Similarly, a local government cannot establish procedures for enactment of zoning ordinances that differ from the procedures outlined in the Enabling Act. ***Rispo Realty v. City of Parma***, 55 Oh.St.3d 101 (1990).

1. **Comprehensive Plan** - The enabling act requires a local government to develop a comprehensive plan. Under traditional zoning plans, property is segregated by use and regulated to control density.

2. **Use** - Traditional zoning establishes single family residential use as the highest classification. Multi-family, commercial and industrial uses are lower classifications. Cumulative Zoning allows a higher use in an area zoned for a lower use, i.e, a single family dwelling in an area zoned for apartment buildings. Non-cumulative zoning restricts an area to a specified use such as industrial use only.

3. **Density** - Density can be controlled by means other than use restrictions. Many ordinances limit building height, set minimum lot sizes or require specified set-back from streets or other buildings. Modern zoning techniques such as "cluster zoning" allow greater building density in one area of a development in return for park space in another.

4. **"Spot Zoning"** - The requirement of a comprehensive plan prevents local zoning authorities from singling out small parcels for either favorable or unfavorable treatment. Spot Zoning is unlawful under the enabling act and may be a taking.

   Example: The local zoning authorities zone two contiguous lots for light industrial use. The surrounding lots are all zoned for single family use. The zoning of the two lots can be challenged as inconsistent with the comprehensive plan.

5. **Variances** - The enabling act authorizes local zoning authorities to grant specific exceptions to the plan known as *variances*. Variances are granted on an individualized basis after a hearing before a body like a board of zoning appeals. To receive a variance, a property owner usually must show that he or she will suffer unnecessary hardship by the enforcement of a use restriction. A lesser standard, practical difficulty, will sometimes justify a variance from a density restriction.

6. **Conditional Uses** - The comprehensive plan sometimes allows zoning authorities to approve inconsistent uses without a showing of hardship. These are usually uses that serve the plan but which are nonconforming. For example, the plan may permit authorities to approve schools in areas zoned residential.

B. CONSTITUTIONAL LIMITATIONS ON ZONING

There are constitutional limitations on the zoning power.

1. **Procedural Due Process** - The due process clause of the Fourteenth Amendment to the United States Constitution requires state and local governments to give landowners affected by a zoning decision **notice** and **opportunity to be heard** before the decision is

implemented. This constitutional right of a landowner to *procedural due process* chiefly affects governments when they act in an adjudicatory as opposed to a legislative capacity.

2. **Substantive Due Process** - Zoning ordinances and regulations must be rationally related to a legitimate governmental purpose. An affected landowner may challenge a zoning ordinance under the Fourteenth Amendment if the ordinance has no such "*rational basis*." The test is very deferential to local zoning authorities.

   Example: A municipality's zoning ordinance limits the height of structures to three stories. Under a rational basis test, the limitation could be justified on the basis that the municipality's fire equipment would have trouble reaching any higher floor.

3. **Equal Protection** - Zoning ordinances have been challenged on the basis of the equal protection clause of the Fourteenth Amendment. Usually the courts apply deferential rational basis test. However, if the zoning ordinance violates a fundamental right or discriminates on the basis of a suspect classification, the court will apply the more stringent "*strict scrutiny*" test. Under this test, the ordinance will be struck down unless the government can show it serves a compelling state purpose and that the ordinance is narrowly tailored to achieve that end.

   Example: A zoning ordinance prohibits yard signs except real estate signs. The locality claims residential signs are a traffic hazard. Because the ordinance impinges upon the right of free expression, a fundamental right, it will receive strict scrutiny. The locality's objective could be achieved by a more narrow ordinance that required signs not to obstruct the view of traffic. ***City of Ladue v. Gilleo,*** 512 U.S. 43 (1994).

4. **Takings** - Actions by zoning officials are frequently challenged as takings under the Fifth and Fourteenth Amendments. A zoning ordinance is particularly subject to challenge if it does not permit a nonconforming use to continue for a reasonable time.

5. **Nonconforming Uses** - A use that does not conform with a newly adopted or amended zoning ordinance must be allowed to continue for a time sufficient to allow the owner to amortize his or her investment in the property. No local government, however, is required to permit a nonconforming use that poses a danger to public health or safety. Moreover, a property owner is not entitled to expand a nonconforming use or rebuild after a casualty loss to continue the use.

   Example: A city enacts a zoning ordinance to bar mobiles home in a given zone. An owner of a mobile home park had thirty mobile homes in his park. After the ordinance is passed, he applies for a certificate to add ten homes to the park. The city could not bar the use of the owner's property for the existing thirty homes but may refuse the application for additional homes. ***Beck v. Springfield Township,*** 88 Oh. App. 3d 443 (1993).

XIII. CONTROL OF LAND USE THROUGH THE LAW OF NUISANCE

A. NUISANCE

The law imposes duties on persons who enjoy rights to property. In general, property owners must use their property in a manner that does not injure the rights of others. (*Sic utere tuo ut alienum non laedas*). A substantial and unreasonable interference with another's use and enjoyment of property is a *nuisance*.

1. **Conduct Required** – A person can be liable for maintaining a nuisance whether he acted intentionally, recklessly or negligently. The courts focus on the harm, not the state of mind of the actor.

   Example: A owns and operates an industrial plant. His dumps waste from the plant into a pit. The waste seeps into the water table polluting his neighbor's well. A is liable to his neighbor for maintaining a nuisance. His dumping of the waste was intentional. The law does not require a person to have the purpose of injuring another in order to be liable for an intentional tort. A would also be liable to his neighbor for the nuisance if the waste polluted the well as a result of an accidental spill. A nuisance caused by negligence is also actionable.

2. **Private Nuisance** – A person injured by another's substantial and unreasonable interference with the person's use and enjoyment of land may bring a private nuisance action. In order to determine whether conduct is a nuisance, the courts today generally apply a *balancing test*. Conduct amounts to an actionable private nuisance if the gravity of the harm suffered by the plaintiff outweighs the utility of the defendant's activity.

   Example: A's house is situated next to a factory owned by B. Soot from the factory occasionally falls on A's house which is one of only a few residences in the area. The soot is not health threatening but does require A to wash his house frequently. The level of soot cannot be reduced by any known technology at a reasonable cost. In weighing the appropriate factors, a court would likely rule B is not maintaining a nuisance. The harm suffered by A is not serious. A's use of his property may not be well suited to the area. B, on the other hand, is engaged in conduct that may be better suited in the area. Moreover, his conduct is socially useful. Preventative measures seem to be impractical.

3. **Public Nuisance** – If a nuisance interferes with rights belonging to the public generally it is called a *public nuisance*. Conduct which threatens the public health, safety, peace or convenience may justify a finding of a public nuisance. The conduct may also involve the violation of a statute or administrative regulation.

4. **Persons Entitled to Bring A Nuisance Action** - Generally, a private party may not bring an action to redress a public nuisance unless the party can show injury beyond that suffered by other members of the public. Public officials may bring an action on behalf of the public at large. Private nuisance actions may be brought by any injured party. The plaintiff in a private nuisance action may be a tenant or the holder of an easement or any other interest in the land.

5. **Defenses** – The defendant in a nuisance action may raise any appropriate defense arising from the law of torts. For example, if a nuisance was caused by the defendant's negligence, the plaintiff's contributory negligence may be a defense.

   A defendant in nuisance action may plead that the plaintiff acquired or improved his property after the defendant began the conduct the plaintiff alleges to be a nuisance. This defense, "coming to the nuisance" is not a bar to the plaintiff's action but rather a factor to be considered by the court in determining whether the defendant's conduct is indeed a nuisance. Similarly, compliance with applicable zoning, environmental, or other land use regulations is not an absolute bar to a nuisance action. The defendant's compliance with these regulations is relevant evidence of the social utility of the defendant's conduct.

6. **Remedies** – The plaintiff who proves the defendant's conduct amounts to an actionable nuisance may recover money damages and seek equitable relief. Traditional equitable doctrines may foreclose equitable relief. For example, a court may find by "*balancing the equities*," that the harm to the plaintiff is serious enough to find an actionable nuisance but limit the plaintiff to an award of money damages because the issuance of an injunction would impose serious hardship on the defendant or others.

Made in the USA
Monee, IL
18 October 2026

66036197R10050